RAND ARROYO CENTER

Sectarianism in the Middle East

Implications for the United States

Heather M. Robinson, Ben Connable, David E. Thaler, Ali G. Scotten

Prepared for the United States Army

For more information on this publication, visit www.rand.org/t/RR1681

Library of Congress Cataloging-in-Publication Data is available for this publication.
ISBN: 978-0-8330-9699-9

Published by the RAND Corporation, Santa Monica, Calif.
© Copyright 2018 RAND Corporation
RAND® is a registered trademark.

Cover: Sunni and Shi'ite Muslims attend prayers during Eid al-Fitr as they mark the end of the fasting month of Ramadan, at the site of a suicide car bomb attack over the weekend at the shopping area of Karrada, in Baghdad, Iraq, July 6, 2016. REUTERS/Thaier Al-Sudani

Support RAND
Make a tax-deductible charitable contribution at
www.rand.org/giving/contribute

www.rand.org

Preface

This report documents research and analysis conducted as part of a project titled *Implications of a Religious War in the Middle East for the U.S. Army* sponsored by Headquarters, Department of the Army, Deputy Chief of Staff, G-8, Army Quadrennial Defense Review Office. The purpose of the project was to examine sectarianism in the Middle East, focusing on Syria and Iraq.

The Project Unique Identification Code (PUIC) for the project that produced this document is HQD146841.

This research was conducted within the RAND Arroyo Center's Strategy, Doctrine, and Resources Program. RAND Arroyo Center, part of the RAND Corporation, is a federally funded research and development center (FFRDC) sponsored by the United States Army.

RAND operates under a "Federal-Wide Assurance" (FWA00003425) and complies with the *Code of Federal Regulations for the Protection of Human Subjects Under United States Law* (45 CFR 46), also known as "the Common Rule," as well as with the implementation guidance set forth in U.S. Department of Defense (DoD) Instruction 3216.02. As applicable, this compliance includes reviews and approvals by RAND's Institutional Review Board (the Human Subjects Protection Committee) and by the U.S. Army. The views of sources utilized in this study are solely their own and do not represent the official policy or position of DoD or the U.S. Government.

Contents

Figures

Summary

This report on sectarianism in the Middle East was written in 2015 with the intent of informing U.S. policy in Iraq and Syria. Since the initial draft was completed, the United States and its allies have defeated the main combat contingent of the Islamic State, the Syrian regime of Bashar al-Assad has rebounded from near defeat, and the Government of Iraq has solidified its control over state territory. While the United States begins to withdraw some of its forces from Syria, tensions between the predominantly Sunni Muslim Saudi Arabian state and the predominantly Shi'a Muslim Islamic Republic of Iran have flared. Many observers of the Middle East perceive an intensifying proxy war between the two heavily sectarian states playing out in Yemen, Syria, and Iraq. War between Saudi and Iranian coalitions seems more likely now than at any point in recent history. Although the analysis and findings in this report date back to 2015, none of the rapidly emerging events in the interim have changed their substance: This report is as relevant today as it was in its earliest draft. What follows is the text from the original report.

Sectarianism in the Middle East

Increasingly, policy decisions are being made based on the assumptions that the Middle East is riven by a purely dualistic sectarian war between Sunni and Shi'a Muslims, that sectarian identity is immutable, and that the underlying sectarian problems in the region are intractable. Following these assumptions, many pundits recommend that the United States not only allow the Middle East to realign to match the sectarian schism but also help reinforce these schisms by supporting the creation of new states and substate regions aligned by sect. Our research shows that the assumptions behind some of these recommendations are often flawed, incomplete, and misleading. While sectarian identity is certainly relevant, it is often less relevant than economic, geographic, political, and other social identities; in most cases, these identities are deeply interwoven. Our research also shows that these sectarian problems are not necessarily intractable: Despite the long history of sectarian divisions in the Middle East, there is also a narrative of cross-sectarian collaboration and supersectarian nationalism. Reinforcing the apparent sectarian rift in the Middle East is likely to undermine rather than further U.S. efforts to stabilize the region. Long-term, strategic success in such places as Syria and Iraq requires a more nuanced understanding of these conflicts and their underlying causes.

While Sunni and Shi'a sectarian conflict in the Middle East spans more than 1,300 years, the nature of sectarianism and sectarian conflict has developed and changed significantly over that time. Contrary to the oft-heard narrative that there is an ancient and continuous history of intractable conflict between the two sects over theological disagreements, a close examination of the interactions between the Sunnis and the Shi'a since their schism shows that political, legal, geographic, economic, ethnic, and other issues have been equally, if not more, important in dividing these groups than the role of theological disagreements. While sectarianism is a driver of conflict in such countries as Iraq and Syria, it would be too simplistic to claim that violence in each country is the result of Sunni-Shi'a religious divisions; rather, geopolitical competition, local disputes, and political rivalries form the core reasons for conflict in each country. Throughout history, these sects have come into conflict more when religion is the primarily expressed identity over other identities, such as ethno-nationalism or local tribal affiliation.

Key Findings

The drivers of conflict between the Sunnis and Shi'a are mostly political in nature, and political and social contexts inform the primacy of sectarian identity and the prevalence of sectarianism. Sectarianism often reemerges in response to a real or perceived threat to resources, security, or adequate representation in a political system. This has especially been the case in the past century, with individuals increasingly desiring a more direct stake in political representation along religious lines, causing sectarianism to become inseparable from the political discourse. When sectarian actors perceive that there is a political threat from another sect due to specific behaviors or rhetoric, there is a tendency to respond in a sectarian manner to protect political and religious interests, and this can lead to a vicious cycle of distrust among the sects.

Sectarianism can best be described as an interrelated but generally two-pronged phenomenon: internal and external. Internal sectarianism occurs at the intrastate level and usually derives from a country's state leaders, religious leaders, or oppositionists who are using sectarian identity for their own political purposes. Top-down pressure has often translated into popular sectarian discord. Historically, sectarian tensions have also flared around sectarian actors' suspicions that other sects are collaborating with foreigners, either sectarian or nonsectarian. Again, this is rooted in a concern that one sect might gain the political upper hand over other sects. In these cases, because of long-standing political concerns, accusations and violent conflict perpetuate further trust erosion between the sects. For U.S. policymakers, foreign internal sectarianism creates a dilemma: Favoritism toward one side of an internal political conflict can backfire, especially if that conflict is based on sectarian divisions. Policymakers should be keenly aware of risk when it proves impossible to remain aloof from an internal sectarian conflict.

External sectarianism takes place on an interstate level and involves a sectarian actor's encouragement of sectarian divisions in foreign countries internally for their own political purposes. This is most commonly seen with state sectarian actors, most recently between Iran and Saudi Arabia. It also takes place between transnational Islamist groups. External sectarian actors exacerbate sectarianism by supporting sectarian sides in regional conflicts. This manifests as a larger geopolitical contest between states or groups portraying themselves as sectarian "champions" to increase their power and regional influence.

Exploitation of sectarian identity tends to exacerbate tensions. One of the main ways sectarian actors involve themselves in conflicts is by appealing to religious identity in their political rhetoric to promote their opposing sectarian brands of Islam. This approach tends to breed sectarian animosity that politicizes the fundamental, but often nonviolent, theological differences between the Sunnis and the Shi'a. The continued politicization of sectarian identity is further exacerbated by the modern speed of communication.

Sectarianism is one of many competing regional identities in the Middle East. In a region where identities are complex, coexisting, and changing, many other individual and group identities can take primary importance over sect. For example, tribal loyalties have trumped religious identity at times when it was more politically expedient or judicious to side with tribe over sect. This could also be said for such other identities as professional, ethnic, or national. Further, Sunni and Shi'a Islam are internally divided along often-important subsectarian lines. Even sectarian state and nonstate actors have to manage these competing identities and deal with the ethnic and religious diversity in and outside of their territory. No actor can operate solely along sectarian lines. Sectarianism is more a political tool than a major driver of conflict, although it seems, with the increased intensity of sectarian rhetoric, that this is changing.

The nature of sectarianism differs significantly by country across the Middle East. Each sectarian conflict, as well as each state in the Middle East region, has a different balance of internally and externally fueled sectarianism. This is partially attributable to the different ethnoreligious composition of each country that results in a unique sectarian and political environment. It is also attributable to the different relationships each state has with external sectarian actors and the different political goals the external actors have in each state or conflict. As is the case with the current conflicts in Syria and Iraq, external sectarianism seems to be more prevalent in Syria, while internal sectarianism has dominated in Iraq.

Iraq suffers from lasting sectarian divisions, but there is nothing inherently intractable or immutable about them. Sectarianism in Iraq can exist alongside nationalism, regionalism, tribalism, and many other "isms" without necessarily causing the disintegration of the Iraqi state. Lasting, if uncomfortable, heterogeneity is possible in Iraq, the way it is in other states. Instead of focusing on sectarianism as a cause of the current problems in Iraq, it would be more effective to think about the intensification of sectarian identity as a consequence of decades of ineffective and oppressive governance and disastrous external interventions. While sectarianism does not necessarily need to dominate the long-term Iraqi political landscape, it seems undeniable that ethnosectarianism will play a strong and perhaps dominant role in Iraqi politics for the foreseeable future. Nearly two centuries of Sunni oppression of the Shi'a will not soon be forgotten, nor will the intense violence of the 2006–2007 civil war or the more recent government oppression of the Sunni. However, the history of sectarianism in Iraq suggests that it is not too late to avert state fragmentation.

The origins of the war in Syria are nonsectarian. The 2011 uprising in Syria was antiregime rather than anti-Alawi (the Alawis being a Shi'a sect). It took on sectarian overtones after external sectarian actors began to offer their support to sides in the conflict that would ensure their political interests. Despite efforts by several parties to exploit sectarian tension to promote their own political agendas, it would be simplistic to refer to sectarian identity as the main source of the uprising against Bashar al-Assad or as the sole motivator of continuing violence. Even now, there are key constituencies inside Syria not motivated by sectarianism.

U.S. policymakers and war planners should avoid oversimplification. Sectarianism manifests itself differently across the Middle East. U.S. decisionmakers should avoid placing people and groups into large, simplified categories for easier identification and, instead, should identify individuals and groups with which the United States can find common ground on political objectives. Sectarianism cannot and should not be eliminated from consideration, but it can be more carefully and effectively situated in policy debates and decisions.

The United States should not choose between Shi'a and Sunni Muslim groups or states. Rather, the U.S. government should be prepared to work with multiple individuals and groups with various sectarian affiliations.

The United States should avoid policies that institutionalize sectarianism. This means working with leaders who are committed to pursuing nonsectarian and pluralistic policies, especially in such places as Iraq where the U.S. military has worked with such individuals. The United States should support and encourage local and state institutions and provide incentives across the sects to achieve participation and inclusiveness in governing institutions.

Acknowledgments

The authors are grateful to the sponsor of this research, Timothy Muchmore, Headquarters, Department of the Army, Deputy Chief of Staff, G-8, Army Quadrennial Defense Review Office. Summer associate Megan Stewart provided a literature review of sectarianism in Syria and Lebanon. We would also like to thank the director of RAND's Army Research Division and Arroyo Center, Tim Bonds; the director of the Strategy, Doctrine, and Resources Center, Sally Sleeper; and our peer reviewers, quality assurance managers, editors, publishing professionals, and graphic artists at RAND.

Abbreviations

AQI	al-Qaeda in Iraq
CIA	U.S. Central Intelligence Agency
CPA	Coalition Provisional Authority
FSA	Free Syrian Army
IDP	internally displaced person
IS	Islamic State
ISCI	Islamic Supreme Council of Iraq
SCIRI	Supreme Council for the Islamic Revolution in Iraq
SoI	Sons of Iraq
UAE	United Arab Emirates
UN	United Nations

CHAPTER ONE

Introduction

This chapter and those that follow were written in 2015. We have limited our modification of the 2015 text to retain the original research. Events through mid-2018 have changed the dynamics on the ground in Iraq and Syria: The Islamic State (IS) caliphate no longer exists as a contiguous, large-scale entity, and IS has devolved from a substantial ground combat organization into a mostly clandestine guerrilla and terrorist force. The emphasis of this work is more on the context of sectarianism to current events than on the events themselves.

This study sought to provide an in-depth historical and contemporary analysis of the nature of sectarianism and what factors drive sectarian conflict in the Middle East, focusing on Iraq and Syria as case studies. Those countries were selected because they are currently experiencing the greatest level of sectarian-influenced conflict in the region. The U.S. military is fighting IS through a sustained air campaign in both Iraq and Syria. While the U.S. Army currently has few combat forces on the ground in the fight against IS, it is crucial that Army leadership understand the sectarian nature of conflict in the region to devise specific policies in fighting groups such as IS.

This chapter provides an introduction to the report, while Chapter Two examines the history of sectarianism in the Middle East to aid our understanding of why sectarianism has worsened in recent decades. Chapter Three examines the history of sectarianism in Iraq and what factors have contributed to internal sectarianism there specifically. Chapter Four provides a similarly in-depth look at sectarianism in Syria. Chapter Five provides conclusions and recommendations for policymakers, scholars, and war planners.

The research here was based on scholarly literature in English but also uses primary regional sources in Arabic and Farsi. In addition, the research utilized domestic and foreign news media analysis, leadership analysis, comparative analysis, and political forecasting.

Sunni-Shi'a tensions in the Middle East have been on the rise for more than a decade. Resurging amid the power vacuum following the U.S. toppling of Saddam Hussein in 2003, sectarianism has increasingly come to be seen as the defining feature of conflicts throughout the region, from Iraq to Syria to Bahrain and Yemen. Numerous analysts now warn that sectarianism has become the biggest source of instability in the Middle East and a growing threat to U.S. interests.[1] However, contrary to the common perception that the regional bloodshed is rooted in a centuries-old dispute over the prophet Mohammed's rightful successor, violent conflict in each country can be found in the current social and political contexts specific to each country and in the way in which communal identity has been manipulated by both local and foreign actors.

Sectarianism refers to the politicization of religious communal identity. One's sectarian affiliation is only one part of one's identity, which also includes national, ethnic, class, and other affiliations. The broader social and political environment greatly influences which facet of identity one asserts. In the 1960s, for instance, ethnic identity dominated politics in the Middle East, as such leaders as Egyptian president Gamal Abd al-Nasser attempted to unify the Arab world based on a pan-Arab identity. With the increase of regional instability during the past decade, sectarian identity has surged as the salience of national identity has waned alongside Arab leaders' growing inability to ensure the security of all citizens.[2] Meanwhile, illustrating the context-specific

---

[1]   See Afshon Ostovar, "Iran Has a Bigger Problem Than the West: Its Sunni Neighbors," *Lawfare Blog*, June 7, 2015; Geneive Abdo, *The New Sectarianism: The Arab Uprisings and the Rebirth of the Shi'a Sunni Divide*, Washington, D.C.: Brookings Institution, 2013.

[2]   Gregory F. Gause, *Beyond Sectarianism: The New Middle East Cold War*, Washington, D.C.: Brookings Institution, 2014.

nature of religious identity is the finding from Pew Research Center polling that many Muslims in East Asia do not even know whether they are Sunni or Shi'a.[3]

Government repression has played a significant role in creating sectarian-based grievances in the Middle East. Because repressive governments do not allow individuals to express their political opinions, many people are forced to organize based on outwardly recognizable identities, such as ethnicity or religion.[4] Furthermore, because people's ideological positions are not known, rulers often simply direct government largesse toward fellow members of their broader kin groups (under the assumption that communal affiliation breeds loyalty). Because religious affiliation tends to overlap with clan affiliation, disenfranchised groups have invariably interpreted government favoritism as being based on sect.[5]

While government oppression and instability have increased the importance of sectarian identity in the Middle East, large-scale sectarian *violence* invariably has been the result of deliberate efforts by domestic and foreign actors to foment social conflict for their own political ends. These "sectarian entrepreneurs" have successfully manipulated latent religious identities to cleave society along communal lines that they can better control.[6] Local politicians, for instance, often have heightened fear of other sects as a means of strengthening control over members of their own religious communities. Leaders also have painted the activities of their opponents as sectarian to dismiss their politically based grievances, often exaggerating their ties to foreign patrons of the

---

[3]   Neha Sahgal, senior researcher, Pew Research Center, "The Escalating Shi'a-Sunni Conflict: Assessing Arab Public Attitudes," conference address, Stimson Center, Washington, D.C., February 18, 2015.

[4]   Justin L. Gengler, "Understanding Sectarianism in the Persian Gulf," in Lawrence G. Potter, ed., *Sectarian Politics in the Persian Gulf*, London: Hurst and Company, 2013, pp. 31–66.

[5]   Madawi al-Rasheed, "Middle East Dictators Feed Sectarianism," *Al-Monitor*, December 15, 2014.

[6]   Toby Dodge, "Seeking to Explain the Rise of Sectarianism in the Middle East: The Case Study of Iraq," Project on Middle East Political Science, March 19, 2014.

same sect.[7] Foreign governments can also take advantage of sectarian grievances to gain inroads among local communities, ultimately exacerbating sectarian conflict in the process. In their rivalry for influence over the region, for instance, Saudi Arabia and Iran support other sectarian regimes, like the Bashar al-Assad regime in Syria, and use militant proxy groups that pursue sectarian goals. In addition, the rise of transnational extremist groups has also precipitated sectarianism regionally. For their part, these groups, such as al-Qaeda in Iraq (AQI), now IS, have been the ultimate sectarian entrepreneurs, targeting the Shi'a with the express goal of stoking sectarian warfare.

Sectarianism exists along a continuum in the Middle East. On one end of the spectrum, people simply fall back on their religious community for protection and other practical considerations. At the other extreme, actions are fueled by hatred based on theology—namely, the belief that members of another community are apostates, or heretics. The proportion of foreign jihadists fighting for theological reasons is greater than that among local fighters, many of whom are pursuing local political objectives.[8] Therefore, the more that sectarian actors and internal grievances have drawn in foreign fighters, the more violent and intractable these conflicts have become. In the case of Iraq, in particular, the internal sectarianism driving conflict has been exacerbated by the role of external sectarian actors, such as Iran and Saudi Arabia.

Posing a significant obstacle to countering sectarian conflict is that regional sectarian actors appear to reject the notion that they have contributed to the problem; Gulf Arab leaders do not see themselves as responsible for spreading sectarian hatred, while the Iranian government does not fully acknowledge how its actions are perceived as sectarian.[9] It is worth noting that, in most of the current conflicts in the region, the majority of foreign fighters animated by religious goals have tended to be Sunni, although large numbers of Shi'a are also active in

---

[7]   Gengler, 2013.

[8]   Fanar Haddad, "Sectarian Relations and Sunni Identity in Post–Civil War Iraq," in Lawrence G. Potter, ed., *Sectarian Politics in the Persian Gulf*, London: Hurst and Company, 2013, pp. 67–115.

[9]   Ostovar, 2015.

Syria and Iraq (particularly if one includes Iranian-backed Shi'a militias operating in Syria). This is largely the result of a strategy employed by numerous Sunni leaders to highlight sectarian divisions to counter what they see as Iran's attempts to establish Shi'a hegemony over the Middle East. Thus, while thousands of Sunni Arabs from the Persian Gulf have traveled to fight in Syria, most of the Shi'a in those countries largely remain focused on attaining rights at home rather than fighting jihad abroad.[10]

For its part, Iran has not employed an overtly anti-Sunni strategy, but rather seeks to downplay sectarian differences so as not to alienate the Sunni-majority population of the Middle East. The Islamic Republic's defense of the Palestinians as Arab Sunnis, for example, as well as its long-standing support to the Sunni militant group Hamas, stand as examples of Iran prizing shared goals over sectarian identity. Tehran's tactical support to Sunni Taliban insurgents fighting U.S. forces in Afghanistan is yet another example.[11] This strategy is a critical component of Iran's effort to overcome the political disadvantage of being a minority-Persian, Shi'a government in a majority-Sunni Arab region.

This is not to say that Tehran has not played a role in fostering sectarianism. While Iran is not opposed to cooperating with Sunnis who share its regional objectives, the majority of "proxy" groups willing to seek Iranian aid are Shi'a groups that tend to believe in (or pay lip service to) the Islamic Republic's religious ideology. Moreover, Iran has attempted (with varying levels of success) to breed loyalty to Supreme Leader Ayatollah Ali Khamenei among Shi'a communities abroad through funding religious foundations and cultural institutes. In the end, Iran's current actions may be more accurately characterized as de facto sectarian—the result of having to rely predominantly on Shi'a groups to gain inroads in the Arab world rather than part of a strategy focused on countering Sunnis.

---

[10] Frederic Wehrey, "The Roots and Future of Sectarianism in the Gulf," Project on Middle East Political Science, March 21, 2014; "Foreign Fighters Flow to Syria," *Washington Post*, October 11, 2014.

[11] Alireza Nader, Ali G. Scotten, Ahmad Rahmani, Robert Stewart, and Leila Mahnad, *Iran's Influence in Afghanistan: Implications for the U.S. Drawdown*, Santa Monica, Calif.: RAND Corporation, RR-616, 2014.

The report's first case study centers on Iraq, a country that, in mid-2015, appeared to be divided along ethno-sectarian lines. Many observers take a reductionist view of the Iraq problem: The Shi'a majority is in control of the government, the Kurds are verging on independence, and the Sunnis are in revolt in the west and northwest. Through this lens, Iraq sits on the regional fault line between Sunni and Shi'a Muslims in the Middle East, and Iraq's slow-motion fragmentation seems to be emblematic of the regional sectarian divide. Chapter Three argues that, in reality, Iraq is more complex and that the reductionist analyses are insufficient and may actually be misleading to policymakers. While many of the overarching assumptions about sectarian divisions in Iraq are accurate, there is a parallel yet interwoven narrative of identity that allows for a deeper understanding of these divisions.

In mid-2015, Arab Muslim Iraqis do tend to emphasize their sectarian identity. Shi'a Iraqis developed a common sectarian identity while suffering through decades of primarily Sunni-led oppression. The Shi'a hierarchy offered a convenient and effective framework for self-defense and for collective action. Sunni Arab Iraqis who had organized along nationalist, Ba'athist, and other nonsectarian lines through 2003 are now struggling to establish a common Sunni polity. However, while sectarianism intensifies in the wake of the 2006–2007 civil war and more-recent government oppression against the Sunnis, other identities remain relevant. These include but are not limited to tribalism, regionalism, and nationalism, with the latter retaining significant relevance even as the country appears on the surface to fragment. In previous decades, all of these competing identities have proven to be resilient and, more importantly, strong influencers on Arab Iraqi behavior. Sunnis and Shi'a have much cause for collaboration and much to dissuade them from state fragmentation.

If Iraq is emblematic of the regional sectarian conflict, it also represents hope for a less sectarian and more collaborative future. Iraq may yet divide along sectarian lines, or it may muddle through to reemerge as a different yet semi-united nation-state. Current crisis makes this nuanced analysis of Iraq less digestible, but understanding this nuance—that extreme sectarianism can coexist with powerful, competing identities, including nationalism—is essential to finding reasonable solutions to the Iraq crisis and perhaps the regional crisis as well.

In Syria, sectarianism is only one of several factors that underlie violent conflict, but its importance appears to be increasing. These other factors—geography and locale, political exigency, class differences, and tribal loyalties—both feed and are fed by sectarianism in Syria. Moreover, Syria's historical foundations do not necessarily render sectarianism in the conflict self-evident. This has led one scholar to term the Syrian war "semisectarian." Both regime supporters and opponents have instigated sectarian-based violence, yet much of the killing of civilians has been indiscriminate (and Sunni IS has massacred Syrian Sunnis who oppose it). But the longer the Syrian conflict continues under the influence of these agendas, the greater the likelihood that parties to the conflict will default to sectarian preferences. This can also be said of Syrian refugees in neighboring countries and across the region, which could increase instability in the region, particularly in Lebanon.

Beginning in 2011 as a nonsectarian revolt against the Bashar al-Assad regime's growing corruption and bad governance, the conflict quickly took on sectarian overtones due to the regime's brutal response, the involvement of external regional actors with conflicting political agendas, and the expanded participation of extremist groups with inherently sectarian ideologies as major combatants in the Syria arena. The regime's strategy was to combine divisiveness based on communal identity with inclusiveness and nationalism depending on the targeted constituency. The regime—whose ultimate goal was survival—sought to magnify sectarian fears among Alawis and Shi'a to maintain a strong constituency, and among Christians and Druze to maintain their neutrality (if not gaining their support). It portrayed itself as a protector of religious moderation and stability against opposing "terrorists." Largely Sunni opposition forces represent a wide array of interests, from nonsectarian moderates (the National Coalition and the Free Syrian Army, or FSA) to violent extremists with inherently sectarian agendas (IS and Jabhat al-Nusra). As radical Sunni jihadist groups have emerged as a more dominant force among the opposition both on the battlefield and in the public eye, so too has a more strident form of sectarianism against Alawis, Shi'a, and other minority groups.

The involvement of Saudi Arabia and Iran and their respective "blocs" in the Syrian conflict is less an originating factor in the uprising and more a catalyst that exploits and fans the increasingly sectarian nature of the conflict in the context of their own geostrategic competition. Sunni Saudi Arabia and Shi'a Iran vie for regional prominence and influence, and this competition has a strong bearing on sectarianism in the Syrian conflict. Saudi and Iranian provision of resources and support to opposing forces in Syria, in combination with calls for Sunni or Shi'a jihad against the other from clerics on both sides, provides fertile ground for reinforcing sectarian trends in the conflict.

But in the midst of heavily publicized acts of sectarian violence and rhetoric, there exist important groups in Syria that are not motivated by sectarianism and do not fit neatly into constituencies ascribed to them by outside observers. Antiregime Alawis, proregime Sunnis, moderate rebel groups, and tribes whose allegiance is based on self-preservation all present counterpoints to what appears to be common wisdom about the Syrian conflict as a "sectarian war." Sectarianism plays an important role in fueling the Syrian conflict, but it has not been the only factor, nor is it uniformly the most important. The conflict is too complex to explain away as a simple explosion of sectarianism with roots in distant history. Allegiances are crosscutting and are based also on political ideology, substate identity, geography and war experience, and economic motivation. However, while caution is warranted in attributing the conflict solely—or even primarily—to sectarian motivations, there is ample reason for concern that sectarianism could lead to worsening of the conflict or to outcomes that do not stop the violence and destabilize the rest of the region.

CHAPTER TWO

The History of Sectarianism in the Middle East

Sectarianism between the Sunnis and the Shi'a is not a modern phenomenon, but it has changed considerably in modern times. Therefore, it is important to examine the 1,300-year history of Sunni-Shi'a sectarian conflict in order to understand what has caused sectarianism to worsen to the heightened level at which it stands today. This historical analysis challenged the oft-heard narrative that a continuous history of ancient and primordial conflict over theological disagreements between the two sects is responsible for the current state of sectarianism in the region. In fact, this interpretation of the history since the Sunni-Shi'a schism asserts that political, legal, geographic, economic, ethnic, and other issues played a role that was equal to, if not more important than, theological disagreements in dividing the Sunnis and Shi'a.

Weighing the salience of sectarian identities to the people of the region is crucial for determining the nature of sectarianism between the Sunni and Shi'a throughout history. Key to this is whether the overall trend during each period of time examined displays that the conflicting sects were identifying primarily on religious lines or whether divisions were driven by theological differences or political, economic, or other issues. It is no surprise that, over time, the Sunnis and Shi'a have come into conflict more when religion is the primarily expressed identity over other identities, such as ethno-nationalism or local tribal affiliation. However, throughout history, the drivers of conflict between the sects have been mostly political in nature—whether that conflict is a struggle against resources and security or for greater representation in a political system. As many scholars have noted, sectarianism is not a constant fight over religious differences but more a reflection of centuries of identity politics being played out between the sects.[1]

It is argued here that a confluence of three factors in the past century have contributed to the rise in sectarianism in the region to its current peak. First, the surge in mass participation in the political processes of the region and an increased desire for a more direct stake in political representation has made sectarianism stronger than it has been at any other time in history. This can be attributed mainly to people asserting religious identity more than in previous centuries as a response to the development of secular nation-states and to the profusion of secular dictators clamping down on political Islam in the region in the past 100 years.

Second, in a further acceleration of the political dimension of sectarian identity politics, the post-1979 and post-2003 environments in the region have seen an even stronger uptick in sectarianism due to increased external encouragement of sectarian divisions. Iran and Saudi Arabia, Shi'a and Sunni, respectively, have used religious identity as a political tool by asserting direct influence in other regional countries' politics in order to promote their opposing political interests. As a senior Shi'a Lebanese cleric, Sayed Ali Fadlullah, remarked,

> Sectarian tools are used in these struggles because they have a greater impact. If you were to call upon people now to fight for a regional or international influence, they won't act. But people will act when it is said that your sect is under threat.[2]

Third, the relatively recent establishment and growing appeal of transnational extremist groups, some with the direct support of state sectarian actors and some without, have further accelerated sectarianism in the region. These groups adhere to an essentialist interpreta-

---

[1]   These include Aslam Farouk-Alli in "Sectarianism in Alawi Syria: Exploring the Paradoxes of Politics and Religion," *Journal of Muslim Minority Affairs*, Vol. 34, No. 3, 2014, pp. 207–226; Vali R. Nasr in *The Shia Revival*, New York: W. W. Norton and Company, 2007; and Karen Armstrong in *Islam: A Short History*, New York: Modern Library, 2002.

[2]   Yaroslav Trofimov, "Sunni-Shiite Conflict Reflects Modern Power Struggle, Not Theological Schism," *Wall Street Journal*, May 14, 2015.

tion of the Quran and espouse deeply sectarian ideologies and policies. These are worrisome trends because sectarianism in the region is being increasingly politicized around the fundamental theological differences between the Sunnis and the Shi'a, making conflict resolution more difficult than before.

Demographics

Demographic realities have played a role in shaping the nature of sectarianism in the region historically. Today, of the 1.6 billion Muslims in the world, Sunnis constitute approximately 85 percent and Shi'a approximately 15 percent.[3] Historically, since Islam was divided between the Sunnis and Shi'a in the late seventh century Sunni Muslims have consistently constituted the majority of the population in the Middle East. As a consequence of their continuous minority status, the Shi'a of the region have experienced more persecution and more pressure to convert than Sunni Muslims. Understanding the sectarian composition of certain societies in the region helps shed light on the interactions between the sects in these places.

The countries in the Middle East with the largest populations of Muslims are Egypt and Iran, one predominantly Sunni and the other Shi'a.[4] The countries with the greatest proportions of Sunnis in their total populations are Egypt, Jordan, and Saudi Arabia, where Sunnis make up around 90 percent (or more) of those populations.[5] There are also substantial majorities of Sunnis in Qatar, the United Arab Emirates (UAE), the Palestinian Territories, Turkey, Afghanistan, and Pakistan, with slight majorities in Yemen, Syria, and Kuwait.[6]

Shi'a Muslims are a majority in the populations of Iran (90 to 95 percent of the population), Iraq (65 to 70 percent), Azerbaijan

---

[3]   "The Future of the Global Muslim Population," Pew Research Center, January 27, 2011.

[4]   "The Future of the Global Muslim Population," 2011.

[5]   "Sunnis and Shi'a in the Middle East," BBC News, December 19, 2013.

[6]   Pew Research Center, "Mapping the Global Muslim Population, Appendix C: Data Sources by Country," October 7, 2009.

Figure 2.1
Shi'a and Sunni Populations in the Middle East

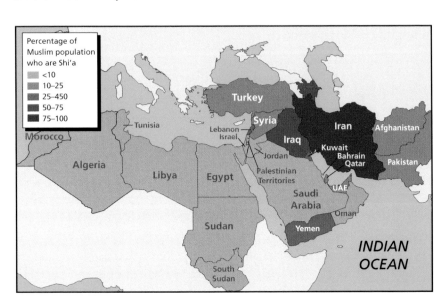

RAND *RR1681-2.1*

(65 to 75 percent), and Bahrain (65 to 75 percent); see Figure 2.1. They have a slight majority in Lebanon (45 to 55 percent) and minority populations in Yemen (35 to 40 percent), Turkey (25 to 30 percent, although most are Alevi Muslims, members of a subdenomination of Shi'ism),[7] Kuwait (20 to 25 percent), Syria (15 percent, mostly Alawi, members of a subdenomination of Shi'ism),[8] Saudi Arabia (10 to 15 percent), Afghanistan (10 to 15 percent), and Pakistan (10 to 15 percent). The largest Shi'a communities in the region are located in Iran (37 to 40 percent of the world's Shi'a), Pakistan (10 to 15 percent), Iraq (11 to 12 percent), Turkey (4 to 6 percent), Yemen (5 percent), and Azerbaijan (3 to 4 percent). The Shi'a populations in these countries

---

[7]   "World Directory of Minorities and Indigenous Peoples—Turkey: Alevis," United Nations (UN) High Commissioner for Refugees, 2008.

[8]   "Syria: International Religious Freedom Report 2006," Washington, D.C., U.S. Department of State, 2006.

constitute roughly 80 percent of the world's Shi'a community, while a significant number of Sunni Muslims reside outside of the region.[9]

Early History and the Sunni-Shi'a Divide

The early history of sectarianism between the Sunnis and the Shi'a is vital in understanding the theological reasons that catalyzed the divide between the two sects, but it also exposes the reality that, as a sectarian conflict, it has always been both political *and* religious in nature, even during the years following the schism, when the theological debate was very active. While sectarianism during this period took place on an individual level as people chose the sect with which they would identify, it manifested mainly on an organizational level between leaders of the religious communities fighting over theology, converts, and territory.

The divide between the Sunnis and the Shi'a is fundamentally about the political succession to the Prophet Mohammed, as well as the questions relating to the qualifications of the successor and the scope of his responsibilities and duties. Mohammed's death in 632 A.D. led to an immediate debate over who would succeed him as ruler of the Muslim community. An elite group of Mohammed's followers selected Abdullah Ibn Abi Qahaafah, known as Abu Bakr, Mohammed's companion and father-in-law, as his successor to run the community as caliph. A minority favored Ali Ibn Abi Talib, the cousin and son-in-law of Mohammed. The majority of the Muslims who followed Abu Bakr became known as the Sunnis, coming from the word *sunna,* meaning "way" in Arabic, and promoted electing caliphs to succeed Mohammed. Those who followed Ali became known as the Shi'a, coming from *shi'atu Ali,* meaning "partisans of Ali," and believed that succession should occur only from Mohammed's bloodline.

In the Rashidun caliphate, the first caliphate after Mohammed's death, the first three caliphs were not directly descended from Mohammed, and the Shi'a lived under their authority but did not view them

---

[9]   Pew Research Center, 2009.

as legitimate. Ali became the fourth caliph in 656, but he ruled for only five years before he was assassinated for his differing views and those of his followers. After his death, the caliphate was ruled by those who defeated Ali and created the Umayyad dynasty (661–750), which held the majority of the lands in the Middle East under its authority. Ali's followers were frequently persecuted and killed throughout this period, but they continued to consider Mohammed's line through Ali to be the rightful lineage of authority, following Ali's son Husseyn as their leader.

The major catalyst for the Sunni-Shi'a schism was the Battle of Karbala, which took place in Iraq in 680. During a clash between Husseyn's followers and the much larger army of the caliphate, the second Umayyad caliph ordered the assassination of Husseyn and his followers. After the death of Husseyn, the Shi'a continued to follow the descendants of Husseyn and Ali in a line of distinctly Shi'a imams[10] as their legitimate religious and political leaders, Ali being the first imam, his eldest son Hassan the second, his younger son Husseyn the third, Husseyn's son Ali the fourth, and so on. To this day, the Battle of Karbala has a highly meaningful place in Shi'a identity. The Shi'a collectively mark the event annually in the commemoration of Ashura. The prevalence of such themes as bravery, martyrdom, and victimization in Shi'a identity can be drawn back to this seminal event that clearly distinguishes Shi'a Muslims as distinct from the Sunnis. After Karbala, the Sunni caliphate continued to reign victorious over the region, and the Shi'a continued to live in varied states of persecution for their beliefs.[11]

---

[10] *Imam* is a general term for an Islamic leader for all Muslims. However, for Shi'a Muslims, the role of an imam is more important because of the concept of *Imamah*, that Shi'a imams have been chosen by God as infallible examples for humanity that all the faithful must follow. Therefore, Shi'a imams play a central role in leading Shi'a Muslims both religiously and politically.

[11] John Morris Roberts and Odd Arne Westad, *The History of the World*, New York: Oxford University Press, 2013, p. 345.

Middle Ages: 800–1500

While early sectarian conflict was initially concerned with practical and theological differences in Islam and people identified primarily along sectarian lines, as the two sects became established, the sectarian division between Sunnis and Shi'a took place less on an individual level and increasingly on a leadership level as political contests for resources, land, and the right to rule continued. Thus, sectarian conflict between the Sunnis and Shi'a worsened in the Middle Ages, particularly during the Sunni Abbasid caliphate (750–1258), which, at its height, controlled all of the Middle East, South Central Asia, and North Africa from its headquarters in Iraq and then Syria. The Abbasid Sunni caliphs brutally cracked down on uprisings by Shi'a communities in their territory for mainly political reasons. They were fearful that there would be a Shi'a reprisal for the death of Husseyn and for the persecution of Shi'a in the caliphate or that the Shi'a would rise up and try to unseat the caliph.[12] The clashes between the Sunnis and the Shi'a during this period can be characterized as increasingly political in nature, as they were not fighting solely for the original theological reasons behind their differences, which were still a significant factor in their conflict, but now also for territory, access to resources, and the right to be ruled under their own sect's interpretation of religious law.[13]

This is perhaps best evidenced by the lives and fates of the early Shi'a imams and their interactions with the Sunnis and their caliphs: By killing Shi'a leaders, the Sunnis could more easily subject the Shi'a to their rule and keep them powerless. According to Shi'a sources, all of the Shi'a imams who lived during this period, from the sixth to the 11th imam,[14] are confirmed or strongly suspected to have been slain or

---

[12] V. Nasr, 2007, p. 53.

[13] Stephen F. Dale, *The Muslim Empires of the Ottomans, Safavids, and Mughals*, New York: Cambridge University Press, 2010.

[14] The 11th imam was the last imam whose life has been recounted in the history. The 12th imam was said to have disappeared in the late ninth century. The majority of Shi'a Muslims today are Twelver Shi'a, meaning that they believe that the 12th imam is the Mahdi, or the one who will return to Earth as the ultimate savior of humanity. Other sects of Shi'ism diverge over opinions on the line of succession of the Shi'a imams.

poisoned on orders of the Sunni caliphs living at the time.[15] The persistence of the Shi'a in continuing to practice under such harsh conditions continued; by the mid–ninth century, the Shi'a had built considerable communities in majority-Sunni areas, such as in Qom and Sabzevar because these areas were isolated enough that the weakening Abbasid caliphate struggled to control them centrally.[16]

Aside from internal sectarian conflict within the large Abbasid caliphate, the rise of a rival Shi'a caliphate from North Africa created intensified sectarianism in the region. The Fatimid caliphate (909–1171) was the only Shi'a-ruled caliphate in the region's history, and it eventually ruled Israel, Lebanon, and western Saudi Arabia, rivaling the Abbasid caliphate as a major regional power. Though the Fatimids were headquartered in Cairo and part of the Ismaili Shi'a sect,[17] they began successfully spreading Shi'a Islam in parts of Abbasid territory and conducting assassinations of Abbasid leaders as an attempt at political subversion.[18] By the middle of the tenth century, caliphs were struggling to rule over the people in their vast swaths of territory and became little more than religious figureheads in practice as local rulers began taking control.[19] In the tenth and 11th centuries, several successful smaller Shi'a dynasties emerged to rule modern-day Iran, Iraq, Syria, and Lebanon.

During this era, caliphates' encouragement of a politicized religious identity and persecution of sects besides their own worsened divisions in these societies and set the precedent for the modern politicization of sectarianism.

---

[15] Sayyid Mohammad Hosayn Tabataba'i, *Shi'ite Islam*, Seyyed Hossein Nasr, trans., New York: State University of New York Press, 1977.

[16] "The Abbasid Dynasty: The Golden Age of Islamic Civilization," Saylor Foundation, 2012.

[17] The Ismaili Shi'a are an offshoot of Shi'a Islam, the members of which believe the line of Shi'a imams should have followed a different person from the seventh imam, rather than the person whom other Shi'a sects believe it followed.

[18] Francis Robinson, *The Cambridge Illustrated History of the Islamic World*, New York: Cambridge University Press, 1996, p. 34; Armstrong, 2002, p. 87.

[19] "The Abbasid Dynasty: The Golden Age of Islamic Civilization," 2012; and Armstrong, 2002, p. xix.

Early Modern Era: 1500–1920

Sectarianism in the early modern period continued to manifest itself mainly as a political contest between regional powers, Shi'a Safavid Persia and the Sunni Ottoman Empire.[20] The Safavid ruler Ismail I, of Turkic descent, was determined to create a Shi'a empire with a separate identity from the Turkish Ottoman Empire. At its height, the Safavids ruled over modern-day Iran and Azerbaijan, the eastern half of Iraq, southeastern Turkey, southwestern Turkmenistan, and the western half of Afghanistan.

In order to establish his empire in a majority-Sunni area, Ismail invited clerics and scholars from major Shi'a centers in Egypt and Lebanon to come to Iran and create a legal system based on Shi'a jurisprudence.[21] The Sunnis living in Safavid territories were forced to convert to Shi'a Islam, and many Sunni clerics and scholars were expelled from the empire or killed, which led to the same reaction against the Shi'a in the Ottoman territories.[22] In many ways, the Safavid-Ottoman rivalry set a precedent for sectarian divisions today, although peaceful coexistence, intermarriage, and cooperation among the Sunnis and Shi'a on local and individual levels were still commonplace despite the attempts of these sectarian powers to create religious divisions for political purposes.

The period of the late 18th and 19th centuries is considered one of relative sectarian stability in the Middle East. Tolerance for other sects became more commonplace as empires declined, less able to govern over large swaths of territory, and tribal and local ethnic affiliations became the more prominent political identity.[23] But under the Tanzimât reforms, the Ottomans developed a new *millet* system through which they gave some autonomy to the non-Sunni sects under

---

[20] V. Nasr, 2007, p. 65.

[21] V. Nasr, 2007, p. 66.

[22] Armstrong, 2002, p. xxiv.

[23] Richard C. Martin, "Empires: Ottoman," in Richard C. Martin, ed., *Encyclopedia of Islam and the Muslim World*, Vol. 1, New York: Macmillan Reference USA, 2004, pp. 214–217.

their rule. This led to greater pluralism, but there was less of an impact on Sunni-Shi'a relations because the Ottomans lumped the Shi'a into the same Muslim *millet* as the Sunnis, failing to recognize them as a separate, legitimate sect.[24] This led to occasional instances of sectarian conflict, particularly when the Ottomans violently cracked down on Shi'a uprisings in the mid-1800s. But there were also other instances of pluralism in the region, as when Nader Shah created the Afsharid Empire in Iran in the mid-1700s based on principles of religious tolerance, as an army of both Sunni and Shi'a Muslims had supported him. Additionally, the region saw more cohesion as identity politics shifted from local and tribal identities to ethno-nationalist identities[25] based on Western ideas of nationalism.

Modern Era: 1900–1979

The fall of the Ottoman Empire was a turning point in Middle East politics; the collapse of the last remaining vestige of centuries of dynastic, imperial rule started an era of mass political participation. Replacing the local, tribal rule that had come to dominate the region in the 19th century, powerful Western states began to divide the previously Ottoman territories into what resembled more "modern" nation-states. The infamous Sykes-Picot Agreement of 1916 determined which areas would be under British or French mandate, with the French controlling upper Syria, Lebanon, and parts of Turkey and the British controlling lower Syria, Iraq, Jordan, Egypt, and Yemen. The British and French organized political representation in each country along sectarian lines, in some cases organizing the political system by confession (Lebanon) and in other cases (Syria and Iraq) splitting the countries into sectarian states. During the mandates, both the British and the French followed a strategy of favoring one sect to administer each country while

---

[24]   Dona J. Stewart, *The Middle East Today: Political, Geographical and Cultural Perspectives*, New York: Routledge, 2013, p. 54.

[25]   S. V. R. Nasr, "European Colonialism and the Emergence of Modern Muslim States," Oxford Islamic Studies Online, 2016.

also encouraging existing sectarian divisions in order to keep the states weak and reliant on their colonial rulers.[26] This practice helped sectarianism take deeper roots in the modern Middle East.

Nevertheless, there was a trend of Sunni and Shi'a cooperation in response to foreign intervention during this period. The Great Syrian Revolt of 1925, an early example of mass political participation in the Middle East, was a collective effort of Syrians across sectarian lines to counter French attempts to divide and rule their country.[27] In Lebanon, the Sunnis and the Shi'a worked together to resist inclusion in the "Greater Lebanon" under domination by Maronite Christians with close ties to the West. In 1943, they agreed to a National Pact under which sects had roughly proportional representation in government.[28] In Iraq, the Sunnis and the Shi'a briefly worked together to drive out British occupation in the 1920s before achieving independence.[29]

This was followed by a widespread pan-Arabist movement, which established political authority under secular authoritarian rulers who emphasized ethnic and national unity instead of narrow sectarian interests. For example, Egyptian president Gamal Abd-al Nasser supported Shi'a clerics against the "corrupt" Shah of Iran and allowed a leading Sunni center for learning, Al-Azhar University, to teach Shi'a jurisprudence starting in 1959.[30] A more aggressive stance against sectarian divisions took place in Ba'athist Syria and Iraq, where leaders were militantly secular and anti-Islamist. In Syria, Hafez al-Assad carefully crafted a culture of national unity by strategically including members of the Sunni majority in key government positions.[31] However, he

---

[26] See Omri Nir, "The Sunni-Shi'i Balance in Light of the War in Syria and Regional Changes," Rubin Center for Research in International Affairs, April 7, 2014; Imad Salamey, *The Government and Politics of Lebanon*, London: Routledge, 2013; and Farouk-Alli, 2014.

[27] Farouk-Alli, 2014, p. 214.

[28] Nir, 2014.

[29] Charles Tripp, *A History of Iraq*, 3rd ed., Cambridge, UK: Cambridge University Press, 2007, pp. 41–42.

[30] Jacques Neriah, "Egypt's Shiite Minority: Between the Egyptian Hammer and the Iranian Anvil," Jerusalem Center for Public Affairs, September 23, 2012.

[31] Reva Bhalla, "Making Sense of the Syrian Crisis," *Stratfor*, May 5, 2011.

also brutally cracked down on Islamist challenges to his rule, as demonstrated by the crushing of Hama's Sunni-led uprising in 1982.

But despite the dominance of secular ethno-nationalist rule, a growing pan-Islamist trend began to bubble beneath the surface among those who favored a stronger place for religion in government. Secular but repressive governance resulted in the rise of an Islamism that would pave the way for the greater sectarianism seen today.

Contemporary Era: 1979–Present

The Iranian revolution of 1979 is, in many ways, the starting point of modern sectarianism in the Middle East. Sectarian divisions became more prominent as regional populations became increasingly dissatisfied living in states without religious ideology or adequate representation across sectarian lines. This was seen most clearly in the Iranian revolution, a mass political movement that unseated Iran's secular shah and established a theocratic Shi'a government. Further, the revolution intensified the regional rivalry between Iran and Saudi Arabia, each of which claimed to be the rightful leader of the Muslim world.

The Iranian revolution became an inspiration for both Shi'a and Sunni Islamists, encouraging many to become more active politically. Iran's new ruler, Ayatollah Ruhollah Khomeini, was charismatic and politically astute: He envisioned Iran having a larger political role in the world and positioned himself not only as a champion of Shi'a Muslims but also as a pan-Islamic leader. Khomeini instituted the concept of *velayat-e faqih* (rule of the supreme jurisprudent) in Iran's constitution, which established the Supreme Leader as the temporal and religious ruler of Iran. This concept would become the basis of Iran's attempts to export the revolution throughout the Middle East.[32]

Inspired by the Iranian revolution, Iraqi Shi'a groups sought to depose Saddam's secular Ba'athist regime.[33] In addition, Iran supported

---

[32]   Christin Marschall, *Iran's Persian Gulf Policy: From Khomeini to Khatami*, New York: Routledge, 2003, pp. 26–27.

[33]   David Gritten, "Long Path to Iraq's Sectarian Split," BBC News, February 25, 2006.

Shi'a groups throughout the region, helping create the Lebanese Shi'a Hezbollah (Party of God), an organization that the United States considers a terrorist group and is closely aligned with Iran, in 1982. But Iran's regional policy was not motivated by purely sectarian objectives, as evidenced by its alliance with Hafez al-Assad's secular and Alawi-dominated regime in Syria. Many Iranian clerics would consider the Alawi sect not as an offshoot of Shi'a Islam but as a heterodox or heretical sect.

The Islamic Republic's assertive foreign policies were viewed with alarm by Arab Sunni authoritarian regimes, particularly Saudi Arabia. There was a growing fear among the Sunnis that the Iranian revolution was a threat to Sunni dominance in the region.[34] In reaction, Saudi Arabia promoted its own Wahhabi creed as a counter to Iran's revolutionary ideology.[35] Saudi Arabia and Iran had been competitors even under the shah's reign, but the Iranian revolution introduced a more sectarian and ideologically driven sense of rivalry between the two.[36] Riyadh's perceived threat of expanding Iranian power and a need to appease the fundamentalist Wahhabi clerics at home led Riyadh to a more assertive regional foreign policy, which espoused radical Sunni Islamism throughout the region.[37]

---

[34] S. Nasr, 2016, pp. 143–144.

[35] Wahhabism is a fundamentalist form of Islam that began in the Arabian Peninsula before the creation of the Saudi state. It promotes the return of Muslims to a literal interpretation of the Quran to cleanse the religion of the mystical and heretical elements that the Wahhabis felt that Islam picked up over time. They believe that all other interpretations of Islam are heretical. The Wahhabis have an important role in the modern Saudi state because of an alliance made between the al Sauds and the Wahhabis to unite the different territories of Arabia into one kingdom. The al Sauds agreed to implement Wahhabi ideology as the kingdom's religion in return for Wahhabi support. In this way, the al Saud royal family still must appease the Wahhabbis to keep the Saudi state together, a difficult feat as the Saudis began to modernize and open Saudi Arabia to the international community

[36] Andrew Scott Cooper, "Showdown at Doha: The Secret Oil Deal That Helped Sink the Shah of Iran," *Middle East Journal*, Vol. 62, No. 4, August 2008, pp. 567–591.

[37] Claude Moniquet, "The Involvement of Salafism/Wahhabism in the Support and Supply of Arms to Rebel Groups Around the World," European Parliament Policy Department, June 11, 2013.

The Saudi-Iranian rivalry is key to understanding the growth of sectarianism in recent years. As Gregory Gause pointed out, Saudi Arabia and Iran did not *cause* the resurgence of sectarianism in the region, but they have certainly exacerbated it to serve their own political interests.[38]

Much of the Middle East experienced relative sectarian peace during the 1980s and 1990s. With some key exceptions, including Saddam's crackdown against the Shi'a following his invasion of Kuwait in 1990, Egypt, Syria, and even Iraq experienced relatively little sectarian violence as the leadership in these countries encouraged ethnonationalist identity rather than sectarianism as the basis of political legitimacy.

Sectarianism has continued to intensify in the past decade with the growing popularity of political Islamism, the recent growth in transnational extremist groups, and the accelerating competition between Iran and Saudi Arabia. Iran's power grew as a result of the U.S. interventions in Afghanistan (2001) and Iraq (2003) and institution of pro-Iranian governments in both countries. U.S. policies had a marked effect on regional power dynamics and Sunni perception of a rising "Shi'a threat." With fewer obstacles to Iranian influence, Tehran has been able to support several nonstate groups in the region, especially Shi'a groups vulnerable to Sunni jihadi violence. Saudi Arabia now sees an Iranian hand in almost every regional conflict, and Iran views Saudi Arabia as an intractable rival. Violent conflict in such places as Iraq and Syria may not have been caused by the Saudi-Iranian rivalry, but the two regional powerhouses continuously feed the flames of war in both countries.

---

[38]   Gause, 2014.

CHAPTER THREE

Sectarianism in Iraq

Iraq is a study in sectarian division, but also in the dynamism and fickle nature of human identity. In 2015, many assumed that Iraqis were, and had always been, on a fixed path toward ethnic and sectarian civil war, that Iraqi nationalism had never been more than a façade, and that the Iraqi state was moving inexorably toward ethno-sectarian devolution.[1] This chapter confirms many of the subordinate assumptions in this overarching forecast, showing how the current Sunni-Shi'a split in Iraq germinated, grew, and was nurtured by the shortsighted actions of various occupying powers. But this chapter also shows how both Sunni and Shi'a Iraqis have previously had, and perhaps retain, the capacity for self-serving yet productive cross-sectarian, and even genuinely nationalist, relationships.[2] It would be wishful thinking in

---

[1]   See, for example, Dawn Brancati, "Can Federalism Stabilize Iraq?" *Washington Quarterly*, Vol. 27, No. 2, 2004, pp. 5–21; Namo Abdulla, "The View from Kurdistan: Divide Iraq in Order to Save It," *Al Jazeera*, June 13, 2014; Ramj Alaaldin, "If Iraq Is to Survive, Then It Must Be Divided into Separate Regions," *Independent*, August 17, 2014; Tim Lister, "Iraq to Split in Three: So Why Not?" CNN, July 8, 2014; Jamsheed K. Choksy and Carol E. B. Choksy, "Defeat ISIS, but Let Iraq Split," *World Affairs*, undated; and Delovan Barwari, "Partition Will Help End the Turmoil in Iraq," *Jerusalem Post*, March 8, 2015.

[2]   Assumptions, findings, and narrative detail for this chapter are derived primarily from Haider Ala Hamoudi, *Negotiating in Civil Conflict: Constitutional Construction and Imperfect Bargaining in Iraq*, Chicago: University of Chicago Press, 2014, Kindle; Hanna Batutu, *The Old Social Classes and the Revolutionary Movement of Iraq*, Princeton, N.J.: Princeton University Press, 1978, Kindle; Dawisha, 2003, 2009; Michael Eppel, *Iraq from Monarchy to Tyranny: From the Hashemites to the Rise of Saddam*, Gainesville, Fla.: University Press of Florida, 2004; Fanar Haddad, *Sectarianism in Iraq: Antagonistic Visions of Unity*, Oxford, UK: Oxford University Press, 2011, Kindle; Kanan Makiya, *Republic of Fear: The Politics of*

2015 to assume that Sunni and Shi'a' Iraqis can soon or easily reconcile. Yet the same historical narrative that explains the current situation also offers hope for eventual, imperfect, but functional national unity.

While many scholars of the Middle East see nuance and subtlety in the evolution of the Sunni-Shi'a relationship, primordialism currently dominates policy debates. For primordialists like Carsten Wieland, Occam's razor cuts through the complexity of Iraqi ethnosectarian identity: If it looks like a three-way ethno-sectarian civil war, it must be so.[3] Other schools of thought present different arguments. Iraq scholar Fanar Haddad takes the ethnosymbolist perspective, but he also makes a more general argument about human identity:[4]

> The fact is that the social and political relevance of sectarian identity [in Iraq] advances and recedes according to wider socioeconomic and political conditions. Likewise, sectarian harmony or division is dictated by context. . . . Perceptions of the sectarian self and other, as indeed with any form of identity, are constantly being renegotiated in what is a perpetually fluctuating dynamic that is neither cyclical nor linear . . . [W]e should begin by recognizing the inherent ambiguity of identity.

Modern Iraq, Berkeley, Calif.: University of California Press, 1989 (1998); Phebe Marr, *The Modern History of Iraq*, Boulder, Colo.: Westview Press, 2012; Yitzhak Nakash, *The Shi'is of Iraq*, Princeton, N.J.: Princeton University Press, 1994; Liora Lukitz, *Iraq: The Search for National Identity*, Portland, Ore.: Frank Cass and Co., 1995; V. Nasr, 2007; Simon, 1986 (2004); Reeva Spector Simon and Eleanor H. Tajirian, eds., *The Creation of Iraq: 1914–1921*, New York: Columbia University Press, 2004, Kindle; Tripp, 2007; and Reidar Visser and Gareth Stansfield, eds., *An Iraq of Its Regions: Cornerstones of a Federal Democracy?* New York: Columbia University Press, 2008. Efraim Karsh, "Geopolitical Determinism: The Origins of the Iran-Iraq War," *Middle East Journal*, Vol. 44, No. 2, 1990, pp. 256–268, and others offer plausible counter- and alternate narratives to the notion that Sunni and Shi'a are caught up in a more-than-1,300-year sectarian rivalry.

[3]   Carsten Wieland, "The Bankruptcy of Humanism? Primordialism Dominates the Agenda of International Politics," *Internationale Politik und Gesellschaft*, 2005, pp. 142–158.

[4]   F. Haddad, 2011, loc. 107, Kindle.

This chapter rejects the simplicity of the primordialist argument without necessarily adopting any other school of thought wholesale.[5] Single-scope analyses can be useful for cutting through complex social issues like those in Iraq, but they also incur significant risk in an effort to simplify a seemingly unmanageable problem. It is enough to say that Iraqis are drawn to multiple simultaneously existing and shifting identities out of fear and a need for human security. Sectarianism is currently dominant, but there is sufficient evidence to show that Iraqis are more complex than bit players in a Manichean sectarian war that appears to many experts to be playing out across the entire Middle East.

This chapter builds from the assumption that Arab Iraqi identities are complex rather than starkly sectarian. It progresses historically and describes the simultaneous descent into sectarianism, as well as the periodic waves of increased "less-sectarian" nationalism throughout the 20th and early 21st centuries. It describes how other issues, including regionalism, tribalism, security, and land rights, affect Iraqi sentiment and behavior to help policymakers identify other factors that stem from or drive conflict. The first part of this chapter summarizes the long and complex history of sectarian division in Iraq, specifically focusing on how modern sectarianism in Iraq takes its roots from the Ottoman period to the Ba'ath revolution in the 1960s. Next it describes how the Arab Socialist Ba'athists, first under Ahmad Hassan al-Bakr and then under Saddam, helped to cement the institutionalization of sectarianism between the Sunnis and the Shi'a. The following section describes the rise of the Shi'a in post-Ba'athist Iraq and the concurrent yet weaker and uneven growth of Sunni Iraqi identity and the impact that it has had on how sectarianism manifests in Iraq today. The final two sections address the implications of the current sectarian divide and forecasts possible futures.

---

[5]   Some of the language used in this chapter will be familiar to constructivists, but the analysis was not applied strictly through a constructionist lens.

Overview

As of mid-2015, Arab Iraqi Muslims found themselves in a de facto sectarian and regional civil war. Cross-sectarian collaboration was limited and appeared to be waning, while cross-sectarian killings and geographic "cleansing" were becoming as common as in the mid-2000s. Shi'a Iraqis representing various political and militant groups led the government from Baghdad and exercised de facto control over the heavily Shi'a regions in the center, south, and east, while Sunnis were in various stages of revolt in the west and northwest.[6] The Shi'a received direct support from Iran based on a historical relationship dating back to the late 18th century, a dynamic we explore throughout the remainder of this chapter. While the Shi'a are currently unified against the Sunni-led threat of IS and against the broader Sunni revolt against the central government, they suffer from considerable internal division along regional and political lines; even in these extreme circumstances, the notion of monolithic sectarian blocs in Iraq is unfounded. The Sunni polity is even more badly fragmented but is in general opposition to what a great number of Sunnis perceive as an unjust Iranian puppet regime in Baghdad.[7] Because many Sunnis believe that they constitute at least half of Iraqis (see following), and because they currently control few economic resources, they have considerable incentive to sustain their revolt until they achieve parity or overmatch with the Iraqi Shi'a.

Sunni sectarian revolt against the Iraqi state is driven by the perception of sectarian and regional repression, by historical expectations of sectarian hegemony, and by basic demands for human security.[8] As of mid-2015, the Iraqi population was estimated to range from 32 to

---

[6]   Kurdish Iraqis anchor the north and northeast, controlling this territory under the Kurdish Regional Government.

[7]   See, for example, Mushreq Abbas, "Iraq's 'Sunni' Rebellion Shows Splits Between ISIS, Others," *Al-Monitor*, June 24, 2014; Dafna H. Rand and Nicholas A. Heras, "Iraq's Sunni Reawakening: How to Defeat ISIS and Save the Country," *Foreign Affairs*, March 16, 2015.

[8]   For definitions and explanations of *human security*, see UN, *Universal Declaration of Human Rights*, December 10, 1948; UN, *International Covenant on Civil and Political Rights: General Comment Number 27—Freedom of Movement (Article 12)*, November 2, 1999; and

35 million people, of whom approximately 75 to 80 percent were Arab and 15 to 20 percent were Kurdish, while Turkmen, Assyrians, and other smaller minorities rounded out the overall population estimates.[9] Ethnic estimates are generally accepted in broad terms, but the sectarian divisions within the estimated 95 to 99 percent of Iraqi Arabs who are Muslims are far more hotly contested. Estimates from generally objective sources range from 32 percent Sunni to 42 percent Sunni and approximately 65 percent to 47 percent Shi'a, out of the approximately 75 to 80 percent Muslim Iraqis who are Arab.[10] However, many Arab Sunni Iraqis and Sunni supporters claim that the Sunnis constitute as much 50 percent or even as much as 62 percent of the *entire* population of Iraq.[11] There are no empirically defensible data to back the

---

UN, *The Human Security Framework and National Human Development Reports: A Review of Experiences and Current Debates*, May 2006.

[9] These estimates are drawn from the UN Department of Economic and Social Affairs and the U.S. Central Intelligence Agency (CIA) World Factbook, which may have drawn from the (also cited) Iraqi Ministry of Planning data; the probability of circular reporting in some of these data sets is high. Because there has been no successful official census in Iraq since 1997, these numbers are extrapolations drawn from multiple sources; see UN, *Data Sources for Population Estimates*, Department of Economic and Social Affairs, Population Division, Population Estimates and Projections Section, 2015b. For estimates, see UN, *Iraq: Population (Thousands), Medium Variant, 1950–2100*, Department of Economic and Social Affairs, Population Division, Population Estimates and Projections Section, 2015a; CIA, "The World Factbook: Iraq," undated; and Republic of Iraq, 2010. For a historical perspective on census analyses in Iraq, see Doris G. Adams, "Current Population Trends in Iraq," *Middle East Journal*, Vol. 10, No. 2, 1956, pp. 151–165.

[10] See, for example, World Values Survey, "Wave 5 2005–2008: Results, Iraq 2006, Technical Record," World Values Survey Association, 2014; Michael Lipka, "The Sunni-Shia Divide: Where They Live, What They Believe and How They View Each Other," Pew Research Center, June 18, 2014; CIA, undated. The World Values Survey data from 2006, with a sample size of 2,701 and an approximately ±3 percent margin of error, showed that respondents identified as Shi'a three times more often than as Sunni, but the question was so poorly written that it should not be used as a basis for further analysis. Note that these data form the basis for some Pew Research Center reports on Shi'a populations in the Middle East. See World Values Survey, 2014, p. 37, and Pew Research Center, 2009.

[11] For example, prominent Iraqi political and religious leaders Mohsen Abdel Hamid, Harith al-Dhari, and Osama al-Nujaifi have all claimed that Sunnis constitute 50 percent or more of the entire Iraqi population. See Shafiq Shuqir, "At-ta'dud al-'araqi wah ad-dini fi bina' 'Iraq al-mustaqbal" [Ethnic and religious diversity in the composition of the future Iraq], *Al-Jazeera*, March 10, 2004; Ayad Mahmud Husayn, "Are the Shia Really the Major-

most-extreme claims, and the more-moderate estimates are, at best, extrapolations from generally poor and dated information. The absence of defensible, objective demographic data undermines accurate analysis, but, even if the data were present, existing and deep-seated cultural narratives might make them irrelevant to the issue of intersectarian tension in Iraq.

Because Iraqis have little reason to trust in official data based on their long experience with abusive and disingenuous governance, and because it is in Sunnis' and Shi'as' immediate and practical benefit to claim a strong majority, cultural perceptions and issues of political advantage are more relevant than objective reality to the present analysis. Distrust and dominance are intrinsically linked and have evolved over the course of at least four centuries. While it has become almost cliché in the fast-moving world of policy analysis to state that the roots of the Sunni-Shi'a split in Iraq are deep, understanding how and why this split emerged—and how it has been temporarily but successfully diminished or overshadowed by other issues in the past—will remain central to finding possible solutions to the current crisis.

Pre-Ba'ath Sectarianism: Challenging Assumptions and Tracing Identities

The state of modern Iraq was created as a kingdom under British mandate in 1921 and was granted independence as a nation-state in 1932.[12] Some leverage these dates and cite Western collusion at various conferences designed to shape Iraq's modern borders to argue or imply that

---

ity in Iraq?" *Al-Arab News*, April 11, 2005; Faruq Ziada, "Is There a Sunni Majority in Iraq?" *counterpunch*, website, December 27, 2006; Abdulaziz al-Mahmud, "New Evidence . . . for the Sunni Majority in Iraq," Defense Network for the Sunnis, March 9, 2010; and Harith al-Qarawee, "The Rise of Sunni Identity in Iraq," *National Interest*, April 5, 2013. Claimants to the 50+-percent figure often cite the 1997 Iraq census, the 2003 UN Ration Card Program review, and 2010 Iraqi Electoral Law as sources for their claims.

[12] Iraq was formed as a mandate state in 1921 and then achieved independence under the Anglo-Iraqi Treaty in 1932. See Marr, 2012, and Abbas Khadim, *Reclaiming Iraq: The 1920 Revolution and the Founding of the Modern State*, Austin, Texas: University of Texas Press, 2012, among others.

the Iraqi nation is an artificiality of the post-Ottoman order.[13] These arguments then conclude that the 1921 state structure has done little more than temporarily repress long-standing enmities between Sunni and Shi'a Arabs who, following the same lines of argument, have lived in separate geographic and cultural cantonments for centuries.[14] Following these arguments, therefore, one might conclude that breaking apart the Iraqi state would allow for naturally occurring stability built on sectarian homogeneity. Ottoman-era provincial divisions, depicted in Figure 3.1, reinforce these assumptions and offer a template for future ethno-sectarian fragmentation.

These assumptions and conclusions are only partly accurate and are, therefore, partly misleading. While the modern state of Iraq did not exist until 1921 (or, officially, 1932), Iraq existed as a region, a group of aggregated provinces, or a semi-amorphous yet state-like entity for well over a millennium under Abbasid, Mongol, and then Ottoman rule.[15] Several scholars make strong arguments that, despite European involvement in the delineation of Iraq's modern borders, the concept of Iraq as a communal region and as a state-like entity long predates the complex series of international and national meetings and agreements that "created" modern Iraq.[16] This matters for the present analy-

---

[13] See, for example, Toby Dodge, *Inventing Iraq: The Failure of Nation Building and a History Denied*, New York: Columbia University Press, 2003.

[14] For example, see Jeffrey Goldberg, "After Iraq," *Atlantic*, 2008; Jeffrey Goldberg, "The New Map of the Middle East," *Atlantic*, June 19, 2014; Toby Dodge, *Iraq: From War to a New Authoritarianism*, London: International Institute for Strategic Studies, 2012; and Sami Zubaida, "The Fragments Imagine the Nation: The Case of Iraq," *International Journal of Middle East Studies*, Vol. 34, 2002, pp. 205–215.

[15] Phebe Marr refers to the Iraqi state under the Abbasid Empire dating from the seventh through 13th centuries, and noted Iraq scholar Abbas Khadim presents compelling evidence that the concept of an Iraqi, and the term *al-Iraq*, emerged as early as the 13th century. See Marr, 2012, p. 5, and Khadim, 2012, p. 7.

[16] See Alistair Northedge, "Al-Iraq al-Arabi: Iraq's Greatest Region in the Pre-Modern Period," in Reidar Visser and Gareth Stansfield, eds., *An Iraq of Its Regions: Cornerstones of a Federal Democracy?* New York: Columbia University Press, 2008a, pp. 151–166; Reidar Visser, "Two Regions of Southern Iraq," in Reidar Visser and Gareth Stansfield, eds., *An Iraq of Its Regions: Cornerstones of a Federal Democracy?* New York: Columbia University Press, 2008a, pp. 27–50; F. Haddad, 2011; and Sara Pursley, "'Lines Drawn on an Empty

Figure 3.1
Ottoman Provinces of Iraq Pre-1916

RAND *RR1681-3.1*

sis because it undermines the argument that the Iraqi state is strictly a modern Western construct artificially stitching together people who would otherwise be naturally segregated by Islamic sect.

Map': Iraq's Borders and the Legend of the Artificial State (Part 1)," *Jadaliyya*, June 2, 2015. Treaties, meetings, and agreements include the 1913 Anglo-Ottoman Convention; the 1916 Sykes-Picot Agreement; the 1920 Treaty of Sevres; the Cairo Conference of 1921; the 1922 (ratified 1930, in effect 1932) Anglo-Iraqi Treaty; the 1922 Uqair Protocol; and the 1923 Treaty of Lausanne. See, among others, Visser, 2008a; "Historical Myths of a Divided Iraq," *Survival: Global Politics and Strategy*, Vol. 50, No. 2, 2008b, pp. 95–106; Richard Schofield, "Borders, Regions and Time: Defining the Iraqi Territorial State," in Reidar Visser and Gareth Stansfield, eds., *An Iraq of Its Regions: Cornerstones of a Federal Democracy?* New York: Columbia University Press, 2008a, pp. 167–204; Marr, 2012; and Khadim, 2012.

Further, Iraqi *nationalist identity* existed well before the 1920 revolution and continues to exist as one of many Iraqi identities.[17] Fanar Haddad, 2011, identified three identity forms held by Iraqi Arabs: unified Iraqi nationalism, Sunni-Iraqi nationalism, and Shi'a Iraqi nationalism.[18] In Haddad's interpretation, all three types of nationalist identity exist simultaneously, but Sunni nationalism and Shi'a nationalism have been in a perpetual state of competition to control the more ephemeral and contested notion of the unified state.[19] Another way to view this dynamic is to see nationalism as a distinct identity that Sunni and Shi'a seek to monopolize or influence. Visser argued that regionalism is another strong identity and that, in *most* cases, regionalism, particularly subprovincial regionalism, influences individual and group behavior more strongly than sectarian identity does.[20]

Another misleading interpretation of Iraqi history persists and feeds current arguments for state fragmentation: the concept that the Sunni-Shi'a split in Iraq is practically timeless, perhaps dating back to the death of the Prophet Mohammed in 632 (or more than 1,300 years prior to the 2015 conflict). While prerevolution Iraq was on the centuries-long front line between the Sunni Ottoman and Shi'a Safavid and Persian Empires, Shi'ism did not proliferate in Iraq until the late 18th century.[21] Up to this point, the Iraqi Arabs were almost entirely Sunni and, in what would become the predominantly Shi'a south in the 19th century, mostly nomadic. Nakash writes, "There is no evidence . . . that the Shi'is were ever close to forming the majority of the population in Iraq before the nineteenth or even the twentieth century."[22] With some effort, one might trace the broad historical dynamic that feeds the current state of civil war back to the origins of

---

[17] Visser, 2008a; F. Haddad, 2011.

[18] F. Haddad, 2011, loc. 737, Kindle.

[19] F. Haddad, 2011, locs. 735–800, Kindle.

[20] Visser, 2008a.

[21] The eternal nature of the Sunni-Shi'a split is implied and perpetuated in most of the profederalist and prodissolution articles cited herein. Nakash and others have provided the historical, primary-source counterargument. See Nakash, 1994, pp. 26–28, among others.

[22] Nakash, 1994, p. 25.

Islam, but, in practical terms, Iraqi sectarianism emerged in the late 18th century as the Ottoman Empire faded from southeast Iraq and Persian Shi'a began to immigrate and proselytize. Therefore, the competition between settled Sunni and Shi'a *in Iraq* is, in practical terms, no more than 200 years old.[23]

Sunni elites in Baghdad—educated, mentored, and nurtured by Sunni Ottomans since the 16th century—saw the Persian Shi'a arrival from the late 18th century through 1920 as a direct threat to their near monopoly over the state.[24] Here, Phebe Marr describes the impact of the Ottoman bureaucracy on Iraqi Sunni and Shi'a perceptions:[25]

> [Under the Ottoman Empire, the] native elite was drawn from only one segment of the population, the urban Sunnis. It was primarily the Sunnis, whether Arab or Kurd, who attended public schools and were given posts in the army and bureaucracy. Not surprisingly, the Sunni came to think of themselves as the country's natural elite and its only trustworthy leaders. Two important segments of the population, the rural tribal groups outside the reach of urban advantages and the Shi'a, were consequently excluded from participation in the government. Little wonder they should form the nucleus of opposition to the government in the early decades of the twentieth century.

In the late 19th century, the Sunni Ottoman developed Sufi orders in the north in order to counteract perceived growth in Shi'a numbers and influence.[26] Shi'a nomads and *fellahin* (farmers), increasingly ostracized by Baghdad through the 19th and early 20th centuries, sought to strengthen their own regional identities. Shi'a *mujtahids*, or recognized religious and political experts on jurisprudence, who were inspired by the Iranian Shi'a revolution, fed this fear both before and after the

---

[23] Nakash, 1994, and others also describe how Shi'ism did not obtain in a significant portion of the Iraqi population until well into the 19th century, coinciding with the mostly forced or induced settlement of the southern tribes.

[24] See, for example, Nakash, 1994; Dawisha, 2003, Kindle; and Marr, 2012.

[25] Marr, 2012, p. 8.

[26] Nakash, 1994, p. 24.

1920 revolution by pressing for a theocratic and presumably Shi'a-led state in Iraq.[27] Beginning in the late 18th century and accelerating in the early 20th century, then, Iraqi Sunni and Shi'a engaged in an evolving tit-for-tat series of exchanges that would incrementally erode trust, strengthen sectarian nationalist identity, and shape the very nature of both Sunni and Shi'a Iraqi interpretations of Islam.

Sunni Identity: 1920 to 1968

This section and the subsequent section on Shi'a identity from the Iraqi revolution against British control in 1920 through the practical beginnings of the Ba'ath era in 1968 present the development of Sunni and Shi'a *sectarian* identities in Iraq. These are the single-scope interpretations of identity leveraged in 2015 to argue for changes in Iraq's state structure.[28] Together, these generally monochromatic narratives show how the current state of distrust evolved (or perhaps devolved) from the prerevolutionary period in a series of path-dependent actions and reactions.[29] The section following the one on Shi'a identity examines alternative identity narratives and injects critical caveats that should inform current analyses.

From the 1920 revolution to the onset of the Ba'ath period in the mid–20th century the Sunni Arab Iraqis retained and reinforced their control over the state apparatus centered in Baghdad. Under British patronage, the Sunni took control of the new Iraqi Army and Parliament, and elements within the Sunni elite increasingly came to view the army as a tool to retain control of the state and to shape Iraqi national identity. Prior to 1920, Ottoman-trained Sunni Arab military and political officers were educated and indoctrinated in the Ottoman

---

[27] A *mujtahid* is a learned religious scholar who, in Shi'ism, has practical and coercive political power. See, for example, Bernard Weiss, "Interpretation in Islamic Law: The Theory of Ijtihād," *American Journal of Comparative Law*, Vol. 22, No. 6, 1978 [*Proceedings of an International Conference on Comparative Law in Salt Lake City Utah*, February 24–25, 1977], pp. 199–212.

[28] Brancati, 2004; Abdulla, 2014; Alaaldin, 2014; Lister, 2014; Choksy and Choksy, undated; Barwari, 2015.

[29] Path dependence is the process of acting in accordance with previously demonstrated behavior rather than deviating to develop new and perhaps more-effective behaviors.

dogma that envisioned the state as strongest when unified and when troublesome ethno-sectarian divisions are minimized. These Sunni elites also retained a residual fear and resentment of Persian influence in Iraq.[30] Existing fears were stoked by the physical presence of tens of thousands of Persian citizens in southern Iraq, as well as the generally mistaken perception that Shi'a politico-religious leaders (primarily clerics) were unified and under the sway or direct control of Iran.[31]

To counter this perceived threat, the Sunni elite centered in Baghdad pressed hard to remove sectarian and even religious identity from the organs of the state to co-opt nationalist identity as a distinctly Sunni, elite identity. At the same time, they moved to settle both Sunni and Shi'a itinerant tribes to reduce the threatening influence of tribal identity and to increase control over the population. They viewed nationalist identity as not only a good unto itself but also a tool with which to keep all Iraqis—and particularly the Persians and Shi'a Iraqis—at bay or under control. As Sunni resentment of the British increased, Sunni elites slewed to German National Socialism and other fascist philosophies as they sought out an alternative patron and an alternative ruling ideology. These strongly nationalist movements further reinforced the Sunni elites' belief that nonsectarian nationalist identity was the key to maintaining centrally controlled state unification, and they fed into the development of Iraqi Ba'athism.[32] Marr writes of the emerging Iraqi dictatorial leanings:[33]

---

[30] Simon, 1986 (2004); Marr, 2012; and the other historians cited herein explain the impact of perceived Persian expansionism and influence. We cite examples throughout this chapter.

[31] Nakash, 1994, cites a range of primary sources explaining how this unity was imagined and never a practical reality. Analysis of modern Shi'a politico-religious organization in the following sections reveals ongoing fissures and a near-total absence of Shi'a political unity.

[32] Reeva Spector Simon explored the inculcation of midcentury German nationalism on the development of Iraqi Sunni military elite and shows how the German-Iraqi relationship accelerated Sunni efforts to unify the state under nonsectarian cultural dictates rather than under a unified version of Islam or as a federal entity (Simon, 1986 [2004]). Also see Lukitz, 1995, pp. 100–101, among others.

[33] Marr, 2012, p. 45.

> A monolithic form of government seemed to offer a more effective means of unifying fragmented countries and modernizing backward societies than did constitutional democracy and the free enterprise system . . . Fascist Italy and Germany in the early days of Adolph Hitler were the models.

Pan-Arab identity and the pan-Arab movement also influenced the development of Sunni Arab Iraqi identity throughout the early to mid-20th century. Pan-Arabism evolved as a structured movement from the 19th century, but it was particularly attractive to some elements within the Sunni Arab Iraqi elite after the 1920 revolution. Pan-Arabism generally aligned with, and mutually reinforced, the Ottoman and German nationalist philosophies and identities in that it argued for supersectarian unity.[34] Reeva Spector Simon and Adeed Dawisha traced pan-Arabist educator Sadi' al-Husri's incorporation of pan-Arabist and nationalist philosophies into the Iraqi civil and military education systems and the subsequent Sunni use of military conscription and forced military education to indoctrinate primarily Sunni Iraqis as extreme nationalists.[35] Al-Husri, a secularist, had particularly strong influence on the development of Sunni Arab Iraqi identity as not only nationalist but also peculiarly nonreligious.[36]

On the surface, then, the Sunni Arab Iraqis who formed the core of the Ba'ath Party in the 1960s and who subsequently benefited from Saddam's presidency were influenced by nearly five centuries of Sunni elitism; they were culturally influenced and educated to expect continuing Sunni domination of the centralized state controlled from the enduring Iraqi capital of Baghdad. Perhaps more importantly, their Sunni identity had very little to do with Sunni interpretations of Islam. While Islam remained important in various aspects of Sunni life and in government, it was eclipsed by Ottoman-, German- , and pan-Arabic–

---

[34] There were also distinct divisions between pan-Arabist Iraqis and nationalists, with nationalists arguing that Iraq mattered more than Arab ethnic identity. While there were differences in the two identities, they both fed Sunni aspirations for centralized power in Baghdad and control over both the state and the Iraqi population.

[35] Simon, 1986 (2004); Dawisha, 2003. Also see Eppel, 2004, pp. 38–39.

[36] Simon, 1986 (2004); Tripp, 2007, pp. 92–93.

influenced nationalism; in many ways, Sunni Arab Iraqi identity was mostly Iraqi, somewhat Arab, and only nominally Sunni. By the late 1960s, the Sunni Arabs had thoroughly rejected British- and American-style democratic ideals, and they had successfully shaped and co-opted the unique philosophies and iconography of the Iraqi state. Because many Sunni elites feared, resented, and, in some cases, looked down on Shi'a Arabs and their Persian influencers, the Sunni leveraged their unique brand of Iraqi nationalist identity to marginalize Shi'a Arabs while periodically buying their loyalty or assuaging their fears with partial participation in government and in the military. Sunni Arab Iraqi identity in 1968, then, appeared to be in direct opposition to Shi'a Arab Iraqi identity and Shi'a aspirations for and interpretations of the state.

Shi'a Identity: 1920–1968

Shi'a Iraqis led the revolution against British control and articulated a vision of a cohesive, Arab, multisectarian state both before and during the revolt.[37] By creating the Sharifian Haras al-Istiqlal (Independence Guard), the Shi'a were able to congregate around a movement that represented both business elites and mujtahids, Shi'a and some Sunni.[38] Despite this (albeit limited) nationalist outreach to Sunni Arab Iraqis, the Shi'a were quickly sidelined in the postrevolutionary process of government formation. After the revolution, Shi'a remained secondary or tertiary partners in governance, and the mujtahids' vision of a more theocratic—though not necessarily Persian-influenced or even Shi'a dominated—state did not materialize. Over the course of the subsequent 48 years, Shi'a Iraqis found themselves increasingly sidelined and, in many cases, violently oppressed by the Sunni-led regime.[39] As the Sunni continued to secularize and nationalize, the

---

[37] Nakash, 1994, pp. 64–77.

[38] Tripp, 2007, pp. 40–41; Simon and Tejirian, 2004, locs. 1003–1016, Kindle. Sharifians were followers of Sharif Husayn Ibn Ali, leader of the anti-Ottoman revolt from 1916 to 1919.

[39] Marr points out that Shi'a probably exceeded Sunni representation in senior government officials during World War II because many Sunni elites were otherwise engaged (Marr,

central and southern Shi'a Arab Iraqis in Najaf, Kut, Karbala, Nasiriya, Diwaniya, and Basra, for example, increasingly came to view Imami Shi'ism as a logical organizing identity for self-defense, for opposition to the unrepresentative central government, and for semi-autonomous self-governance.[40]

Unlike Sunnism, which generally envisions a personal relationship between worshipper and God, Iraqi Shi'ism organized around imams and mujtahids. As in Iran, this allowed for the formation of a structured, hierarchical framework that, in turn, gave the Shi'a considerable ability to organize and to maintain control over political and religious messaging. Further, the Shi'a narrative of manhood and victimhood originating in the legacies of Ali and Husseyn provided a useful backdrop and corollary for continuing victimhood at the hands of the central government and even via external assaults from Sunni Wahhabi tribes pressing north from what is now Saudi Arabia.[41] Therefore, while Iraqi Sunnism became less important as a religious identity and perhaps secondary or tertiary in terms of a politico-religious identity, Shi'ism became increasingly important and cohesive while the southern Iraqis remained in opposition.[42]

Sunni elites' fear of Shi'a opposition led to a series of legal and military actions against Shi'a mujtahids and political leadership throughout this period. In several instances, the central government expelled Shi'a mujtahids, forcing them to Iran and therefore somewhat closer to the Iranians.[43] While this did strengthen the relationship between Iranian and Iraqi Shi'a, Yitzhak Nakash, 1994, argues, it did not homog-

---

2012, p. 57). Nakash, 1994, Marr, 2012, and Adeed Dawisha, *Iraq: A Political History*, Princeton, N.J.: Princeton University Press, 2009, Kindle, all carefully document the degradation of the relationship between the Sunni central elites and the Shi'a southerners.

[40] Nakash, 1994, and others contend that there are significant differences between Iraqi and Persian Shi'ism, and that Iraqi Imami Shi'ism differs in both political and religious context from Persian (Iranian) Shi'ism.

[41] Nakash, 1994, p. 78.

[42] This occurred despite the relative weaknesses in the Iraqi Shi'a *waqf*, or religious endowment, in comparison with the Iranian Shi'a *waqf*. See Nakash, 1994.

[43] Nakash, 1994, pp. 82–83.

enize cross-border Shi'ism. Instead, Iraqi Shi'a retained their unique precepts and perspectives. The power and influence of the mujtahids ebbed and flowed through 1968, but, by the time the Ba'athists came to power, the Shi'a religious and political networks in the south were essentially one and the same. While Shi'a religious identity flourished, it merged with regional identity in the same way that Iraqi Sunnism merged with nationalist identity.[44]

Many Shi'a dabbled in alternative identities throughout the post-1920 period. Iraqi communism emerged in the late 1920s in Shi'a-dominated Basra and Nasiriya and gradually evolved to include Kurds and Arab Sunnis, primarily in Kirkuk and Baghdad. Ultimately, a number of the Iraqi Communist Party's (ICP's) leftist precepts were co-opted by the Sunni-dominated state. The ICP emerged as a social movement driven by anticolonialism and class struggle, and it remained at least partly aloof from the churning sectarian issues that emerged and evolved throughout the 20th century. Shi'a who formed or joined the ICP retained their Shi'a identities, but the most-prominent members claimed primary allegiance to the party. A primordialist would classify ICP activity as a diversion from the essential nature of Iraqi Arab Shi'ism. Alternatively, the cross-ethnicity, cross-sectarian ICP not only offered a different organizing identity but also demonstrated Shi'a willingness to find common cause with non-Arab, non-Shi'a Iraqis.[45]

After the 1920 revolution, or uprising, the other major turning point in Shi'a identity through 1968 occurred after the 1958 Free Officers' coup. In what Marr, 2012, termed the Shi'a revival in Iraq, mujtahids and other Shi'a leaders rapidly expanded their opposition to state repression under the dictatorship of Sunni Arab Iraqi president Abd al-Karim Qasim. Marr writes, "The intense secularism of the regime and its support for leftist policies soon provoked a reaction from conservative Shi'i elements and a religious revival among Shi'i youth."[46]

---

[44] Visser, 2008a, p. 18.

[45] Ilario Salucci, *A People's History of Iraq: The Iraqi Communist Party, Workers' Movements, and the Left 1924–2004*, Chicago: Haymarket Books, 2003 (tr. 2005), provides a detailed description of ICP evolution and activities.

[46] Marr, 2012, p. 103.

Opposition activists formed the southern Shi'a Da'wa (Call) Party, led by Muhammad Baqr al-Sadr, the father-in-law of contemporary Iraqi politician and militia leader Muqtada al-Sadr.[47] Formation of Da'wa solidified several elements of the long-standing Shi'a opposition into what would be an enduring and powerful, primarily sectarian political force that would eventually fracture into several competing Shi'a political movements, including the Supreme Council for the Islamic Revolution in Iraq (SCIRI). This dynamic of surface-level sectarian unification paralleled by severe and sometimes violent internal division would continue in both the Sunni and Shi'a camps through 2015.

Understanding of Iraqi Identity from 1920 to 1968

Both of these sectarian identity narratives are generally accurate, and the mutual sense of mistrust developed from 1920 through 1968 does provide an important part of the general framework for viewing the current Sunni-Shi'a divide. However, several other factors shape what could be a more nuanced analysis of Iraqi identity in the pre-Ba'ath era. First, a range of competing identities was sustained, developed, or emerged during this same period. Tribalism predates Islam and was only slightly diminished by settlement, institutionalization, and ethno-sectarian unification.[48] Regionalism, closely associated with tribalism—tribes tend to exist as at least semihomogeneous entities in most rural areas—also persisted as a critical Iraqi identity. Most Iraqis included, and continue to include, either a tribal or regional *nisba*, or the equivalent of a Western surname, in their formal names, both indicating and reinforcing tribal and regional identification.[49] Other competing identities also affected decisionmaking, including urban versus rural residency. This was particularly relevant for Sunni elites in Baghdad, who often viewed themselves as superior to both Shi'a *and* Sunni

---

[47] See Patrick Cockburn, *Muqtada: Muqtada al-Sadr, the Shia Revival, and the Struggle for Iraq*, New York: Scribner, 2008; Tripp, 2007, and Marr, 2012, among others.

[48] See Judith Yaphe, "Tribalism in Iraq, the Old and the New," *Middle East Policy*, Vol. 7, No. 3, 2000, pp. 51–58; and Nakash, 2003, among others.

[49] See Beth Notzon and Gail Nesom, "The Arabic Naming System," *Science Editor*, Vol. 28, No. 1, 2005, for a lay explanation of Arabic naming conventions.

farmers, and for southern Shi'a, who resentfully viewed urbanized Iraqis as, in one characterization, an *effendi* class who had adopted suspect Western attitudes.[50] Yaphe, 2000; Khadim, 2012; Nakash, 1994; Visser, 2008a; and most other historians cited in this chapter provide significant evidence that tribal and regional identities strongly influenced individual decisionmaking and group behavior during the 1920 revolution and at various times through 1968.[51] While it would not be possible to make an empirical argument that tribalism or regionalism trumped sect in any one place or time, empirical evidence that sectarian identity trumped tribal or regional identity in individual decisionmaking is equally absent. As noted in the previous section, *communist* also emerged as a significant political identity beginning with a tiny student movement in 1924 and peaking in the late 1950s.[52] Communists and their political leaders played important roles in major events throughout the 20th century, and communist Iraqi Sunni and Shi'a Arabs and Kurds showed how Iraqis could organize around an alternative social and political identity.[53]

Sectarian identity became an anchor point for a great deal of interregional competition, but practical, economic issues like land ownership and access to services also drove decisionmaking throughout the 1920–1968 period. Central government officials in Baghdad generated a cascading series of economic setbacks for southern, primarily Shi'a Iraqis when they passed the 1932 Land Settlement Law[54] and

---

[50] *Effendi* describes educated, wealthy notables in various Middle Eastern and Mediterranean societies. In this case, the Shi'a probably used the term to associate urban Sunni elites with the Ottomans. See, for example, Lukitz, 1995, p. 133.

[51] Visser, 2008a.

[52] See Dawisha, 2003; Salucci, 2003 (2005); F. Haddad, 2011; and Marr, 2012.

[53] John F. Devlin, "The Baath Party: Rise and Metamorphosis," *American Historical Review*, Vol. 96, No. 5, 1991, pp. 1396–1407; Salucci, 2003 (2005); F. Haddad, 2011; Marr, 2012. Haddad describes how Iraqi pan-Arabists used the Iraqi communists' connection with Iranian Tudeh communists to label the Iraqi travelers as "un-Arab." See F. Haddad, 2011, loc. 945, Kindle.

[54] "Lazma Law No. 51 of 1932," *Iraq Government Gazette*, No. 23, June 5, 1932, pp. 423–424.

the redistributionist 1958 Agrarian Reform Law,[55] the latter of which became a tool for land appropriation.[56] Southern Iraqi Shi'a Arabs who had any stake in land ownership probably based their future decisions in part on their reactions to this social and economic policy. In effect, therefore, *landowner* was a viable Iraqi identity that could coexist with Shi'a, southerner, or other identities, and any landowner might act against the prevailing interests of sectarian leaders at any point in time. The idea that Iraqis would act against the interests of de facto or de jure sectarian leaders is overlooked in more surface-level treatments of Iraqi identity, but Nakash, Marr, Dawisha, and other historians show that these diversions were commonplace.

Lastly, but perhaps most importantly for present analyses, there were periods of genuine, large-scale, cross-sectarian unity, countless incidents of more individual-level cross-sectarian collaboration, and many incidents of intrasectarian division throughout the period in question. The first and most prominent event of collaboration was the 1920 revolution against the British occupation. Southern Arab Shi'a Iraqis initiated the revolt and constituted the majority of the fighters who had success against the British as far north as Hilla, while Sunni opposition was more compartmented. However, Khadim, 2012; Nakash, 1994; and others describe how Shi'a and Sunni collaborated against the British in an overarching, generally nonsectarian, yet also informal nationalist movement. While there were many subsequent low points in cross-sectarian unity, particularly from the mid-1940s through the mid-1950s as the Sunnis consolidated their control of the state, the Iraqi Ba'ath Party was, at its origins, a genuinely cross-sectarian organization. At least eight prominent founding members, including Fu'ad al-Rikabi and Ali Salih al-Sa'adi, were Shi'a Iraqi Ba'athists who helped both empower and transform the party from a fledgling enterprise into a ruling elite in just under two decades.[57] Divisions

---

[55] Government of Iraq, "Agrarian Reform Law of the Republic of Iraq," No. 30, Baghdad, Iraq, October 1958.

[56] See, for example, Marr, 2012, p. 41.

[57] See Dawisha, 2009, p. 174; and Marr, 2012, pp. 114–115, among others. Rikabi left the party in 1963 (Dawisha, 2003, p. 224).

within the sects were rife throughout the 1920–1968 period. For example, Dawisha describes how election rigging and the passage of a universal conscription law in 1934 led several prominent Sunni leaders to consider overthrowing the government; later coups and countercoups all revealed deep intrasectarian division.[58]

Ba'ath-Era Sectarianism and Other "-isms"

Iraqi Ba'athists maintained unbroken control of the state from the 1968 coup to the 2003 U.S.-led coalition invasion, first under the coleadership of al-Bakr and Saddam, and then from 1979 to 2003 under Saddam alone. Ba'athist ideology, imagined in the 1940s in Syria as a high-minded vehicle for unity, freedom, and socialism, was quickly co-opted as paranoid anti-*shu'ubiyin* nationalism.[59] By 1968, in Iraq, Ba'athism had fully morphed into a stridently nationalist and functionally fascist and secular identity.[60] By the early 1970s, Iraqi Ba'athism had become little more than an organizing identity that primarily Tikriti Sunni Arab Iraqis used to centralize authority, stifle resistance, and exert control over the arms of government and the population. Some Shi'a remained Ba'athists but only to retain a few existing positions of power, to serve as well-compensated ministerial and parliamentary tokens for rural southern Shi'a, or because the alternative to party membership was exclusion from all other lucrative government opportunities. Iraqi Ba'athism branched sharply away from Syrian Ba'athism, which the Sunni Iraqi Ba'athists came to associate with Iranian Shi'ism and Iranian geopolitical expansionism. Enmity between Sunni Arab Iraqi Ba'athists and Shi'a Iranians would not only continue to grow but would flourish under the al-Bakr-Saddam regime,

---

[58] Dawisha, 2009, loc. 671, Kindle.

[59] *Shu'ubiya* was a term used by Ba'athists as a straw man or perhaps bogeyman, representing Shi'a, non-Ba'athists, Persians, Westerners, or anyone else not in agreement with Ba'athist ideology. *Shu'ubiyin* is one loose transliteration for individual shu'ubiya (Makiya, 1989, pp. 216–220).

[60] Devlin, 1991; Marr, 2012; Tripp, 2007, pp. 183–228; Makiya, 1989 (1998), p. 16.

and then explode into all-out war after Saddam seized power in 1979. This ongoing external struggle, rooted in the centuries-old Ottoman-Safavid conflict, would continue to influence relations between Sunni and Shi'a Iraqis and concurrently harden sectarian divisions within the state. However, as in the 1920–1968 period, alternative explanations for behavior and alternative identity theories are also relevant to understanding sectarianism under Ba'athist rule.

Shi'a in Opposition and Revolt

While some Shi'a Arab Iraqis were Ba'athists, served in the army, or avoided sectarian political activity, the paranoia and repression of the primarily Sunni Ba'athists would eventually impel the Shi'a to revolt. As al-Bakr and Saddam cracked down on the Sunni in Anbar and elsewhere, tightening control of the party structure and bringing the historically troublesome officer corps into line, Sunni elites continued to view the south, and more broadly the Shi'a, as the central threat to the regime. Another sweeping land reform decree passed in 1969 (after the 1932 and 1958 laws) seemed designed to sow distrust within the Shi'a community, revealing the leading edge of what some analysts view as the Ba'athists' anti-southern, anti-Shi'a agenda.[61] The 1979 Iranian revolution accelerated Sunni Ba'athist paranoia, particularly as Saddam ousted al-Bakr and assumed control of the state; al-Bakr was more moderate toward the Shi'a than Saddam was.[62] Arrests, sham trials, expulsions, and executions of key Shi'a leaders hardened antigovernment (and therefore anti-Ba'athist, anti-Sunni) sentiment. Crackdowns on Shi'a religious ceremonies and the targeting of the Shi'a religious leadership—and particularly the 1980 arrest, torture, and killing of Muhammad Baqr al-Sadr—would harden Shi'a opposition, strengthen

---

[61] Amatzia Baram noted that this decree also led to the seizure of large portions of some Sunni-held land. This led to violence with primarily the Jubbur tribe (Amatzia Baram, "Neotribalism in Iraq: Saddam Hussein's Tribal Policies 1991–1996," *International Journal of Middle East Studies*, No. 29, 1997, pp. 1–31, pp. 4–6).

[62] Marr, 2012, pp. 177–178.

the Da'wa party's draw, and set the stage for eventual intrasectarian fractures between Da'wa and the Sadrists.[63]

Dawisha argues that Saddam saw Da'wa as "an advance bridge-head for the [Iranian] ayatollahs' ambitions in Iraq [and as] a mortal danger to his political order."[64] In Saddam's interpretation, he invaded Iran primarily out of sectarian fear and animus, spurred by the 1979–1980 Shi'a demonstrations, riots, and assassinations of Ba'athist officials. But other scholars, including Karsh, 1990, and Tripp, 2007, have argued that nationalism and geopolitical rivalry featured more prominently in Saddam's decisionmaking. In this interpretation, nationalist identity and practical need, or perhaps greed, were the primary drivers of violent behavior, not sectarian animosity. Whatever the reasons for the Iraqi invasion, the 1980–1988 Iran-Iraq War would help both to solidify the practical aspects of the Sunni-Shi'a rivalry and to convince many politicians and scholars that the centuries-old, Ottoman-Safavid, regional Sunni-Shi'a rift was not only ongoing but accelerating.

Formation of the anti-Ba'athist Badr Corps in the early 1980s would have long-reaching consequences for all Iraqis. Throughout the remainder of the Ba'athist period, the geopolitical maneuvering between Iraq and Iran would have strong sectarian overtones, and the actual tit-for-tat actions taken by both sides even after the end of the Iran-Iraq War (including covert infiltration and direct violence) would continue to fuel sectarian fears. In Saddam's paranoid mind, the Shi'a were Persian agents, while the Iranian *marjaiyeh* viewed the Ba'athist Sunni Arab Iraqis as embodying secularism, anti-Shi'ism, and Arab nationalism.[65] This ongoing external hot and cold war with Iran inflamed and hardened sectarian fears and identities in both Sunni and Shi'a camps in Iraq.

From 1980 through 2003, Saddam and his Ba'athist Sunni Arab Iraqi subordinates wavered back and forth between anti-Shi'a violence and rather thinly veiled efforts to sustain and build what Fanar Haddad, 2011, calls Shi'a nationalism. This often included manipulation of Shi'a

---

[63] Marr, 2012, pp. 170–175.

[64] Dawisha, 2009, loc. 4147, Kindle.

[65] *Marjaiyeh* refers to Iran's religious leadership.

tribal identity, an aspect of southern Arab Iraqi identity often over-looked in contemporary analyses.[66] During the Iran-Iraq War, Saddam made an effort to show he was religious, and his government increased donations to the Shi'a *waqf* to encourage Shi'a volunteerism.[67] Indeed, many thousands of Shi'a Arab Iraqi soldiers fought against Iran, partly because they were conscripted and threatened but perhaps also in part out of nationalist zeal. By the mid-1990s, this partly manufactured cross-sectarian sentiment had all but disappeared at the national level. The post–Gulf War, SCIRI-inspired, Badr Corps–led intifada in 1991 was, according to Nakash, 1994; Marr, 2012; and other scholars, gen-erally a Shi'a sectarian revolt against the Ba'athist Sunni Arab state.[68] Even though some Shi'a supported the government and abstained from participating, the failure of the revolt and the brutal repression that followed further hardened southern Shi'a Arab identity and opposi-tion to the state.[69] Marr writes, "Among the Shi'i population of the south, alienation from the regime was higher than at any time since the founding of the state."[70] By the mid-1990s, the Ba'athists had fully co-opted nationalism for their own uses and transformed it into some-thing unattainable for Shi'a outside of the co-opted Shi'a Ba'athists. While Saddam continued to try to co-opt the Shi'a, primarily leverag-ing tribal rather than sectarian or nationalist values, his actions and policies made clear his true intentions.[71] In the wake of the intifada, the

---

[66] Baram, 1997, accurately treats tribalism as a separate identity that is relevant to all Arab Iraqis.

[67] Makiya, 1989, and others make convincing arguments that this newfound religiosity was a practical tool for repression and state consolidation rather than a genuine reflection of belief in Sunni or broader Islamic teachings.

[68] This was also a Kurdish and partly Sunni revolt. All of the various uprisings in Iraq were complex, and most crossed ethno-sectarian lines in some way or another. Because this report deals with Arab Sunni-Shi'a conflict, this chapter does not expressly touch on Kurdish par-ticipation in various events.

[69] Baram, 1997, pp. 8–9.

[70] Marr, 2012, p. 232.

[71] For example, see Baram, 1997, p. 20.

Shi'a mujtahids and politicians accelerated efforts to recast nationalism in terms relevant for southern Shi'a Arabs.

Sunni, Tribal, and Military Identities Within the Ba'athist State

Throughout the Ba'athist period, the Sunni elites in Baghdad and Tikrit strengthened their overall control of the state using brutality, intimidation, torture, and pervasive state security measures.[72] While the Shi'a and Kurds suffered most directly under Saddam, the central Ba'athist authorities also had a complex relationship with the Sunni Arab population in the west and northwest. Saddam and his top leadership viewed the Sunni fellahin, tribal leaders, and lower-middle class in the center and central north as a threat to the state. Baram and others describe both al-Bakr's and Saddam's efforts to eliminate, or at least weaken, tribal identity across Iraq. These efforts generally failed, and instead Saddam co-opted tribal leadership and leveraged tribal law and identity to his own ends.[73] Sunni military officers, most of whom had some Ba'athist affiliation, were also a continual source of trouble for the regime. While the military had been co-opted and controlled by the Ba'athists, long-running Sunni Arab efforts to leverage the military as a nationalist force also generated considerable pride in military service. *Military officer* continued to be an Iraqi identity unto itself, and it was one that frightened Saddam and senior nonmilitary Ba'athists.[74]

---

[72] See Makiya, 1989 (1998); Tripp, 2007; Marr, 2012; Dawisha, "'Identity' and Political Survival in Saddam's Iraq," *Middle East Journal*, Vol. 53, No. 4, 1999; and F. Haddad, 2011, among others.

[73] Keiko Sakai, "Tribalization as a Tool of State Control in Iraq: Observations on the Army, the Cabinets and the National Assembly," in Faleh Abdul-Jabar and Hosham Dawood, *Tribes and Power: Nationalism and Ethnicity in the Middle East*, London: Saqi Books, 2003, pp. 109–135; Hosham Dawood, "The 'State-ization' of the Tribe and the Tribalization of the State: The Case of Iraq," in Faleh Abdul-Jabar and Hosham Dawood, *Tribes and Power: Nationalism and Ethnicity in the Middle East*, London: Saqi Books, 2003, pp. 83–108; and Faleh A. Jabar, "Sheikhs and Ideologues: Deconstruction and Reconstruction of Tribes Under Patrimonial Totalitarianism in Iraq, 1968–1998," in Faleh Abdul-Jabar and Hosham Dawood, *Tribes and Power: Nationalism and Ethnicity in the Middle East*, London: Saqi Books, 2003, pp. 53–81, provide the best description of this effort and its outcome. Also see Baram, 1997, p. 3.

[74] Jabar, 2003, pp. 80–81.

This identity was further mixed with Naqshabandi Sufism, an order or practice that transcends religious identity boundaries and has become closely linked with post-2003 antiregime sentiment.[75] After Saddam's fall, this mix of Ba'athist, nationalist, Anbari-Ninewi, tribal, and Sufi identity would take on as much importance as Shi'a nationalist, tribal, and southern regional identities.

Western Sunni Arabs in Anbar Province, the primary recruiting pool for the Sunni Arab military, had a long history of fickleness toward centralized control. Saddam was equally fickle in his treatment of the Sunnis in the periphery, and, in 1995, some Anbaris staged a significant revolt against the state.[76] What began as a small movement spread quickly to include Sunni Arabs from both the Dulaymi and Shammar tribal confederations and members of the Iraqi Army.[77] Sunni Arabs in Anbar, technically cosectarians with Saddam, rallied around tribal identity and their own interpretation of nationalist identity. In a foreshadowing of the series of Anbari-led movements in the post-2003 period, Sunni Anbaris formed the Armed Dulaymi Tribe's Sons Movement. Despite support from a rebellious Republican Guard Army unit, this revolt was violently defeated.[78] In the revolt's wake, Saddam increased efforts to co-opt tribal identity, rearranging tribal leadership under a new (1996) High Council of Tribal Chiefs. This led to the creation of what U.S. officials in the post-2003 period often referred to as "fake sheikhs," so called because they claimed lineage or authority they did not possess. However, while tribal identity was simultaneously weakened and co-opted during the Ba'athist period, tribal iden-

---

[75] Michael Knights, "The JRTN Movement and Iraq's Next Insurgency," West Point, N.Y.: Combating Terrorism Center, 2011; Quil Lawrence, "U.S. Sees New Threat in Iraq from Sufi Sect," National Public Radio, June 17, 2009.

[76] Baram, 1997, p. 6; David Wurmser, *Tyranny's Ally: America's Failure to Defeat Saddam Hussein*, Washington, D.C.: American Enterprise Institute Press, 1999.

[77] Anbar Province is the former Dulaym Province, named for the central geographic distribution of the loosely associated tribal confederation. Many Shammar also live in Anbar, and many Dulaymis are closely related to Shammar in other parts of Iraq and across the region.

[78] Wurmser, 1999, provides one of the best descriptions of this revolt. The citations in Baram, 1997, are the most exhaustive, although nearly all references to this uprising are from secondary rather than primary sources.

tity would continue to either dilute or reinforce sectarianism as identities merged and morphed in the wake of the 2003 invasion.

Post-Ba'ath Sectarianism

As with the pre-2003 period, there are two ways to view post-2003 sectarianism. A starkly sectarian interpretation paints a dire picture of rapid and perhaps irrecoverable state and social disintegration driven by, and in turn hardening, long-standing religious divisions between Sunni and Shi'a Arabs. Many elements of this interpretation are accurate, and, in the chaos of the occupation period, sectarian identity in its various forms did play a significant and, in many cases, overriding role in shaping individual and group behavior. However, for the most part, Arab Iraqis split on sectarian lines because sect provides the most convenient and useful "level" of identity; in practicality, this was also a regional civil war between west-northwest and center-south-southeast. Regionally aligned sectarianism became an organizational vehicle for collective self-defense.

Fanar Haddad described how sectarian identity can shift from banality and passivity to take on a dominant and aggressive form.[79] Toby Dodge, 2012, argued that this is exactly what occurred in the aftermath of the invasion. Alternative analysis blends together various identities, including sect, tribe, region, insurgent group, political party, landowner, military officer, and, perhaps most importantly, Iraqi nationalist. This lens of analysis offers greater hope for the future of Iraq, but there is perhaps an equal or greater argument to be made that the hardening of sectarian identity in the post-Ba'ath era, and the leveraging of sectarian identity to justify extreme violence, have pushed Arab Muslim Iraqis beyond the point of national reconciliation.

A snapshot of the overarching sectarian dynamics after 2003 offers a stark picture for the present and future of Iraq. Operation Iraqi Freedom completely, and in all likelihood permanently, upset the centuries-old power relationships within the Arab Iraqi community.

---

[79] F. Haddad, 2011, p. 25.

Through 2003, the Sunni elites mentored, shepherded, and empowered by the Ottomans and the British retained some or nearly all control of state authority. Sunni military officers, fellahin, urban laborers, tribal elders, and business executives had been conditioned to expect not only indirect, nominal control of the state but also most of the privileges and benefits that came with power and control. The impact of this cultural expectation-shaping cannot be overstated: Most Sunni deeply believe not only that they are privileged to control Iraq but that (as explained in the first part of this chapter) their numbers far exceed the most-likely estimates of the actual Arab Sunni population. The Sunnis' fall from power was rapid, shocking, and, as this chapter describes, strictly unacceptable to people so deeply conditioned to the status quo.[80] On the other hand, the Shi'a, shaped by approximately 200 years in subordinate opposition, by the religious and historic narratives of victimization, and by very real and recent experiences with Ba'athist Sunni violent oppression, were perhaps unnecessarily graceless in victory. While some thoughtful Shi'a, including Grand Ayatollah Ali al-Sistani, sought a stable peace and even reconciliation, some of the Shi'a who assumed control of the state reportedly adopted the most-inhumane Ba'athist Sunni tactics—including sectarian cleansing, torture, and murder—to retain state control. This placed the disorganized Sunnis in what appears to be perpetual opposition to the state they once controlled.

Sunni Realign in Opposition

In both his 2011 book *Sectarianism in Iraq: Antagonistic Visions of Unity* and his 2014 article "Reinventing Sunni Identity in Iraq After 2003," Fanar Haddad laid out a precise, well-reasoned, and plausible explanation of the Sunni Arab Iraqi response to the system shock of the invasion. He argued that, prior to 2003, there was no Sunni Arab Iraqi identity to speak of, at least not in religious sectarian terms. *Sunni* was one of many descriptors an Arab Iraqi might use for self-identification, rather than a deeply held, belief-driven identity. Iraqi

---

[80]   See, for example, Fanar Haddad, "Reinventing Sunni Identity in Iraq After 2003," *Current Trends in Islamist Ideology*, Vol. 17, 2014, pp. 70–101, p. 81.

Sunnism had been so thoroughly enmeshed with, isolated from, or co-opted by nationalism, pan-Arabism, tribalism, and Ba'athism that it no longer had distinct substantive meaning. Because the Sunnis had been in control of the state for so long, they had never been pressured to generate effective group organization for self-preservation or opposition.[81] After the invasion and the dissolution of both the Sunni-dominated government and the security services, all Arab Iraqis who were also Sunnis were effectively thrust into the unfamiliar and uncomfortable position of powerless minority.[82]

In the rural areas of the predominantly Sunni provinces of Anbar, Nineweh, and Salah al-Din, many Sunni Arab Iraqis immediately reverted to tribal identity.[83] Tribal identity was particularly convenient for local self-organization and self-defense because it was immediately available and because, in the mid- to late 1990s, the tribes had obtained substantial arms—including artillery—from the regime and from illicit activities.[84] But as it became apparent that the Shi'a were taking control of the reins of state power, it was increasingly necessary to organize above tribal level. Because the Sunni-dominated Ba'ath Party was decimated and overtly banned, and because the Sunnis had no real or widespread practice in political organization, the Sunnis consistently failed to organize around an even remotely cohesive or broadly representative political movement. Authority figures with genuine coercive power and popular draw among some elements of the Sunni polity tended to be high-level Ba'athists who were legally excluded from the political process following the passage of the Coalition Provisional

---

[81] F. Haddad, 2014, p. 74. Tribal and regional identities far superseded Sunni sectarian identity in the Ba'athist era. See, for example, Baram, 1997.

[82] Dodge, 2012, describes this process in plain and convincing detail.

[83] See, for example, Gary W. Montgomery and Timothy S. McWilliams, eds., *Al-Anbar Awakening Volume II: Iraqi Perspectives from Insurgency to Counterinsurgency in Iraq, 2004–2009*, Quantico, Va.: Marine Corps University Press, 2009.

[84] Baram, 1997, and Dodge, 2012, both describe how the mid- to late-1990s dynamics between the regime and tribal elders led to the distribution or acquisition of weaponry.

Authority (CPA) Order 1.[85] Dodge, 2012, describes the failure of the Iraqi Islamic Party (Hezb al-Islami al-Iraqiyeh) and the Iraq Accord Front (Jibhet al-Tawafuq al-Iraqiyeh) to generate any real grassroots support, even considering various political successes. In the absence of political organization, and in the face of increasing political disenchantment and social violence, Sunni Arab Iraqi identity gradually hardened and then evolved from 2003 through 2015.

It took several years for Sunnis to identify as Sunni. At first, national representatives were reluctant to frame any issue in sectarian terms.[86] This was due at least in part to the aggressive efforts dating back to the Ottomans, and later al-Husri and the Ba'athists, to remove sectarianism from Iraq's national lexicon; acknowledgment of sectarianism was generally viewed as benefiting Shi'a and Persian rather than Sunni nationalist narratives.[87] Over time, many Sunnis, and particularly those Sunnis who had self-selected or were assigned as political representatives, began to adopt the pre-2003 Shi'a narrative of victimhood. They almost precisely, if perhaps unintentionally, reversed roles with the Shi'a whom the elite Ba'athist Sunnis had once repressed.[88] This sense of isolation and victimhood was reinforced by external actors (more on that later), by the continuing failure of Sunni political elites, and by the increasingly paranoid and aggressive Shi'a-led government that enacted policies and supported actions that, like the Ba'athist policies of the previous era, seemed tailor-made to evoke aggressive opposition.

Despite considerable efforts by the U.S.-led coalition to reduce sectarian discord, by the end of the U.S.-led occupation in December 2011, many Sunnis believed that they had been almost completely disenfranchised from the state.[89] The results of the 2010 parliamentary

---

[85] CPA, "Coalition Provisional Authority Order Number 1: De-Ba'athification of Iraqi Society," Baghdad, Iraq, 2003.

[86] F. Haddad, 2014, pp. 81–82.

[87] F. Haddad, 2014, p. 97, among others.

[88] F. Haddad, 2014, p. 82.

[89] Priyanka Boghani, "In Their Own Words: Sunnis on Their Treatment in Maliki's Iraq," Public Broadcasting Service, October 28, 2014; Kurt Sowell, "Iraq's Second Sunni Insur-

elections, which effectively cemented Shi'a control of the government, proved to be the last straw for Sunnis who, after seven years of ineffective self-organization and revolt, were beginning to coalesce at the grassroots level around a series of mostly justifiable grievances.[90] The Iraqi Army, which, according to Dodge, had refrained from participating in the sectarian civil conflict in 2006, was being picked apart and refilled with loyal but generally incompetent Shi'a officers. The army, which had, for so long, been a bastion of Sunni pride and power, was transforming into a symbol of anti-Sunni repression. Opposition was particularly strong in the 99-percent Sunni province of Anbar, which received comparatively little of the oil-funded largesse handed out in Baghdad, the south, and the Kurdish areas and which suffered considerably throughout the 2003–2008 insurgency.

Beginning in 2012, Sunni Arab Iraqis in Anbar, Kirkuk, and Nineweh Provinces began a long-running series of social and political protests against the Baghdad regime led by then–prime minister Nuri al-Maliki. These protests culminated in violent clashes in Hawija in early 2013 and then an aggressive clampdown on protestors in Ramadi in late 2013.[91] By early 2014, Anbar Province was in full revolt, and IS had seized Fallujah and other parts of Anbar. By the summer, Mosul was under IS control, and the Iraqi Army had all but collapsed in the west and northwest. As of 2015, Sunni politicians had either been expelled or become generally irrelevant in the state decisionmaking process. The Sunnis continued to articulate their victimhood at the hands of the Shi'a state, and now at the hands of increasingly confident Shi'a militias. Simultaneously, they refused to accept their minority status. Nonetheless, social media data in Anbar Province in 2013 and 2014 revealed an almost complete absence of sectarian propaganda. Instead, the Sunnis in Anbar framed their revolt against the state in

---

gency," Hudson Institute, 2014.

[90]   See Ben Connable, "A Long Term Strategy for a Democratic Iraq," *War on the Rocks*, June 30, 2014, for a list of these grievances.

[91]   See, for example, Tim Arango, "Dozens Killed in Battles Across Iraq as Sunnis Escalate Protests Against Government," *New York Times*, April 23, 2013; and Kamal Namaa, "Fighting Erupts as Iraq Police Break up Sunni Protest Camp," Reuters, December 30, 2013.

historical, nationalist terms, evoking images of Saddam and retaining their claim on Baghdad.[92] Sunni identity may be emerging in Iraq, but, at least as of mid-2015, it remained tightly entwined with nationalist and regional identities.

Shi'a Struggle to Define a Cohesive and Inclusive Majority Identity

On the verge of the U.S.-led invasion in 2003, the southern Shi'a Arab Iraqis, who probably constituted a sizable majority of the national population, were more than ready to help expel the Ba'athists from power. Shi'a nationalism, in Fanar Haddad's construct, had completely diverged from the Ba'athist Sunni articulation of nationalist identity.[93] When military actions destroyed the Iraqi state, it presented a nearly clean slate from which the Shi'a, initially empowered by the CPA, could begin to reverse their perpetual misfortune and assume control of the state as a genuine (if not empirically proven) majority. Unlike the Sunnis, the Shi'a already had a robust sectarian identity they could attach to and leverage to assume control of the government and the security services. Nearly two centuries of constant pressure from the Sunni-led state had forced together the Shi'a *hawza* and political movements, deeply intertwining sectarian with political, regional, and (their interpretation of) nationalist identity. Unfortunately, three factors would hinder, and in some ways cripple, what might have been a triumphant and successful righting of the sectarian balance in Iraq.

First, the Shi'a had been so violently and ruthlessly oppressed for so long that they possessed an understandably deep-seated mistrust and hatred of the elite Ba'athist Sunnis.[94] Some Shi'a were able to compartmentalize these sentiments and allow for the idea of a unified ethno-sectarian state, continuing the widespread grassroots-level interactions and communalism with Arab Sunnis, Kurds, and other Iraq-

---

[92] This finding is derived from a structured analysis of selected months of Twitter data from al-Anbar Province posted online between December 2013 and August 2014.

[93] F. Haddad, 2011; V. Nasr, 2007.

[94] Marr, 2012, p. 300.

is.[95] However, a significant number of Shi'a elites saw the 2003 reversal as an opportunity to unify and benefit the Shi'a at the expense of the Sunnis. In turn, many Sunni Arabs played into the hands of the most aggressive and paranoid of these Shi'a leaders by adopting anti-Shi'a rhetoric and participating in intersectarian violence.[96] Some of the first instances of sectarian cleansing came from the Sunni Arab refugees from Fallujah in 2004 as they fled into western Baghdad and began attacking Shi'a residents. This gave Shi'a leaders the excuse to at first suppress, and then repress and disenfranchise the Sunnis.

Second, the Shi'a had little to no experience in governance. While many Shi'a were Ba'athists and held high positions in government and the military, these Shi'a were generally excluded from the post-2003 political process. There were very few Shi'a politicians in the emerging Shi'a elites who could claim expertise in senior leadership or management positions. As a result, the first decade of Shi'a-dominated governance was messy, inefficient, and corrupt. Political patronage took on greater importance than governance. This general lack of competence and overt patronage to the fractured Shi'a political class simply reinforced Sunni Arab perceptions that the Shi'a Arabs were incapable of leading the Iraqi state. This in turn reinforced the enduring Sunni Arab nationalist, but countergovernment, agenda.

Third, despite the relatively greater cohesion of Shi'a Arab Iraqi identity compared with that of Sunni Arab Iraqi identity, the Shi'a were still badly fractured and remained so in mid-2015.[97] Old divisions between Da'wa, SCIRI, and the Sadrists came to full fruition in the wake of the invasion. Muqtada al-Sadr was able to co-opt a version of Shi'a identity, leveraging what Visser, 2008a, and Nakash, 1994, aptly describe as a type of Shi'a regionalism, in Sadr's case centered on Najaf

---

[95] Anecdotal evidence of these recent cross-sectarian relations was presented to one of the authors of this report during multiple research interviews for an ongoing RAND project between 2013 and 2015. Also, Sunni militias fought alongside Shi'a militias and the Shi'a-dominated Iraqi Army in Anbar Province in 2015.

[96] F. Haddad, 2013.

[97] See Marr, 2012, pp. 308–310, among others.

and Karbala.[98] SCIRI, transformed into the Islamic Supreme Council of Iraq (ISCI), leveraged the Badr Corps to gain and maintain power through 2010. Both Shi'a and Sunnis came to see ISCI and Badr as a thinly veiled extension of Iranian identity and influence in Iraq, which turned off even some hard-core Shi'a Arab sectarians. Further, ISCI's support base is in Basra; Basrawis tend to be federalists rather than nationalists, and this regional identity colors ISCI's political and sectarian policies.[99] ISCI and Da'wa forged a semi-unified political front to lead Iraq under Prime Minister al-Maliki, and now under Haider al-Abadi, but Da'wa has overshadowed ISCI since the 2010 elections. This intrasectarian miasma reveals not only the fractures within Shi'a political identity but also the underlying regional and external identity narratives that influence Shi'a Arab Iraqi behavior.

Al-Maliki, a Shi'a Arab from a district near Karbala, Iraq, was elected with U.S. support in 2006 and retained control of the state through mid-2014. In his first few years in office, Maliki made a number of overt and aggressive efforts to both assuage Sunni fears and to rein in Sadr and other Shi'a he viewed as dangerous malcontents. His initial statements in office in 2006 and 2007 probably helped to influence many Sunnis to take a chance on the Awakening Movement that helped to reverse the AQI-dominated Sunni insurgency.[100] In 2008, the Maliki-led government passed the Provisional Powers Act, which granted some authority to provincial governments; this was a clear effort both to address Sunni complaints and to help channel some of the ongoing Shi'a city-regional activism in the south.[101] Maliki's 2008 "Charge of the Knights" into Basra was designed to rein in Sadr and, perhaps as a secondary objective, to demonstrate Maliki's resolve to form a unified, ethno-sectarian state.[102] However, as relations with the United States began to sour after 2008, Maliki articulated

[98] See V. Nasr, 2007; Cockburn, 2008; Marr, 2012; and Dodge, 2012.

[99] See, for example, Visser, 2008a.

[100] See, for example, Montgomery and McWilliams, 2009.

[101] See Marr, 2012, p. 322, among others.

[102] See Marr, 2012, pp. 322–323, among others.

his policies in increasingly sectarian terms. He directly undermined and, in some cases, attacked the post-Awakening Sunni militias, undoing the cross-sectarian goodwill developed from mid-2006 through 2008. Alienation of the Sunnis accelerated after the U.S. withdrawal in December 2011, and, by mid-2014, both elite and grassroots Sunni Arab Iraqis had come to see Maliki as not only a vehemently anti-Sunni leader but also a tool of Iranian anti-Arab and anti-Sunni activities.

As of mid-2015, the Shi'a-led state has proven unable to extend genuine reconciliation opportunities to the Sunni.[103] Hopes that the new prime minister al-Abadi would be able to reverse Maliki's sectarian policies foundered in great part because Abadi was increasingly beholden to Iranian leaders who, it appeared, were happy to allow the Sunni Arab Iraqis to remain in revolt.[104] Shi'a identity continues to play a centralizing and safeguarding role for Shi'a Arabs in Baghdad and across the south and southeast, but it has also evolved into an identity of political and social dominance that appears increasingly at odds with Sunni Arab Iraqi identity. The rise of Shi'a militias to counter IS threatens not only to alter Shi'a Arab Iraqi identity but also to thrust it toward anti-Sunni militancy. What remains unclear is the degree to which Arab Iraqis living in central, southern, and eastern Iraq, most of whom happen to be Shi'a, will be amenable to national reconciliation over time.

External Influence: The United States, Iran, and the Gulf States Influence Iraqi Identity

In retrospect, it is difficult to view U.S. involvement in post-2003 Iraqi identity politics as anything but harmful. The first acts of the CPA, including de-Ba'athification, the dissolution of the Sunni-dominated army, and the elevation and inclusion of unpopular expatriate Shi'a

---

[103] Despite several announcements since assuming office in 2014, Prime Minister al-Abadi had been unable (as of mid-2015) to enact major reforms that might further reconciliation. An August 2015 anticorruption measure did not directly address Sunni grievances. See Haider al-Abadi, "PM's First Package of Reforms to COM," official text, Government of Iraq, August 9, 2015.

[104] Sunni revolt in western and northwestern Iraq would allow increased Iranian intervention in Iraq and Shi'a leaders affiliated with Iran to increase their influence over time.

figures into the governing process, gave the immediate and forceful impression that the invasion and occupation were designed to remove Sunni Arab Iraqis from power and influence.[105] De-Ba'athification and the dissolution of the army also unintentionally gave the impression that the CPA was punishing all Sunnis for the past transgressions of the Sunni elite. With the assistance and influence of the UN and other external influencers, the CPA then brokered the formation of the Iraqi Interim Government under Ayad Alawi, a Shi'a with cross-sectarian popularity.

Ayed Alawi may have been an acceptable candidate to lead Iraq, but, by taking a strictly ethno-sectarian approach to divvying up authority within the Iraqi Governing Council, the United States and its partners encouraged Iraqis to harden identities along ethno-sectarian lines.[106] This affected all Iraqis, but the composition of the ICG—13 Shi'a, five Sunni, and five Kurds, one Turkman, and one Assyrian—made Shi'a majority and Sunni minority an official reality.[107] Well after the dissolution of the CPA, coalition leaders continued to try to stabilize Iraq by supporting what seemed to be equitable power distributions along ethno-sectarian lines, forcibly imposing the best-guess estimates of Iraqi population data on an unwilling Sunni polity. Shi'a politicians leveraged these U.S. policies to control the state, which, in turn, inflamed both anti-Shi'a and anti-U.S. sentiment among the Sunnis.

Worse still, U.S. policy and apparent favoritism toward the Shi'a wavered as the insurgency gained momentum and Sunnis challenged the new status quo.[108] U.S. military and political leaders began to court the Sunnis and tried to rein in Shi'a political leaders and Shi'a security force and militia leaders. This apparent fickleness hardened sectarian identity as Shi'a leaders began to feel isolated from the United States and therefore more vulnerable to Sunni revanchists. Direct U.S. support to the Sunni Arab Awakening Movement and formation of Sons

---

[105] See, for example, CPA 2003.

[106] Tripp, 2007, pp. 267–286; Marr, 2012, pp. 288–345.

[107] F. Haddad, 2011, loc. 3214, Kindle.

[108] See Marr, 2012, pp. 296–331, among others.

of Iraq (SoI) militias, which generated approximately 100,000 armed members, led some Shi'a to believe that the United States was naively giving the Sunnis the means to overthrow the Shi'a state.[109] These militias also harkened back to the Sunni elites' use of National Guard militia units to oppress the Shi'a in the 20th century.[110] Maliki's anti-Awakening and anti-SoI actions were probably intended to assuage both his own fears and the concerns of his constituents.

Discussed in more detail later in this report, sectarian activity in Iraq incited by regional state actors like Iran, Saudi Arabia, and the states of the Cooperation Council for the Arab States of the Gulf has been equally disruptive, although far less equitable toward the Sunnis, Kurds, and other Iraqis, as that of the United States and the UN. Seen through a geopolitical lens, Iranian concerns with Iraq date back to the Ottoman-Safavid conflict. Contemporary Iranian policy on Iraq began to emerge in the early 20th century as the new Iraqi government began to expel Iranian citizens who had been living in southern Iraq. In the latter part of the 20th century, Iran supported the development of SCIRI and the Badr Corps to influence Iraqi politics and to help undermine the Ba'athist state. In practical terms, Iran has been directly involved in covert, clandestine, and overt political warfare in Iraq since the 1980s.[111] After 2003, Iranian leaders simply leveraged SCIRI (then ISCI) and Badr to influence Iraq from inside the new government. They also helped to inflame the anti-U.S. insurgency by arming Shi'a militias with heavy rockets and advanced improvised explosive devices, further driving the United States away from the Shi'a at the height of the insurgency.[112] Iranian support to the Shi'a and the presence of Iranian advisers and business professionals in Baghdad gave the Sunni a rallying cry in opposition. To the more-militant Sunnis, and then to many at the grassroots level, Shi'a became "Safavids," and Iraqi Shi'a

---

[109] See Marr, 2012, p. 310, among others.

[110] See, for example, Dawisha, 2009, loc. 3431, Kindle.

[111] See, for example, Joseph Felter and Brian Fishman, *Iranian Strategy in Iraq: Politics and "Other Means,"* West Point, N.Y.: Combating Terrorism Center, U.S. Military Academy, October 13, 2008.

[112] Felter and Fishman, 2008.

became "puppets of Iran."[113] As of mid-2015, Iran had an overt military presence across north-central Iraq, and it appears that the Iraqi government places more confidence in Iranian than in U.S. support.[114] Direct Iranian support for openly anti-Sunni militias like Asa'ib Ahl al-Haq has led many Sunni Arab Iraqis to believe that Iran is intent on helping Iraqi Shi'a to cleanse Iraq of its Sunni population.[115] As with U.S. actions in Iraq, nearly all Iranian actions have been either unintentionally or, in this case, intentionally harmful to Sunnis and other minorities.

Gulf Sunni Arab involvement in Iraq has, perhaps, been equally harmful. While Gulf involvement in Iraq has been far murkier than U.S. and Iranian involvement, there is evidence to show that wealthy Gulf donors and some states provided direct support to Sunni insurgents.[116] Motivations for this support were probably varied, but many Gulf leaders and analysts view the ongoing war in Iraq both as a central struggle between Sunnis and Shi'a and as a potential proxy war between Sunni Arabs and Shi'a Iranians. If the Gulf Sunni Arabs can help sustain an anti-Shi'a Iraqi revolt, and perhaps even overthrow the Shi'a-led, Iran-backed regime, Iran will be set back and will have less influence over the Gulf and less opportunity to threaten Arab Gulf states. While this analysis requires some supposition, it fits within the overt rhetoric found in open-source data.[117]

---

[113] These terms and associated images emerged consistently in a review of publicly available Twitter postings from Sunni areas of Iraq from late 2013 to late 2014.

[114] Michael Knights, Philip Smyth, and Ahmad Ali, "Iranian Influence in Iraq: Between Balancing and Hezbollahzation?" Washington, D.C.: Washington Institute, June 21, 2015.

[115] This sentiment was revealed to the chapter author by Sunni Iraqi interlocutors in a series of interviews, emails, and informal discussions between December 2013 and August 2015.

[116] See, for example, "Saudis Reportedly Funding Iraqi Sunni Insurgents," *USAToday*, December 8, 2006.

[117] These assumptions are reinforced by an extensive review of public Twitter data, news reports, and Iraqi-generated YouTube videos from December 2013 through August 2015.

Intersectarian Violence and Its Impact on Identity

Invasion plunged Iraq into a continuous cycle of high-intensity and low-intensity violence ongoing through mid-2015. Rationales behind violent actions are complex and differ from act to act and target to target. A significant amount of Sunni and Shi'a violence between 2003 and 2008 was directed at coalition forces and may have been only remotely or incidentally influenced by sectarianism. However, beginning in mid-2004, Sunni Arab Iraqis and Shi'a Arab Iraqis began to target each other with increasing frequency. By mid-2006, Dodge, 2012, and others argue, Iraq was in the midst of a full-blown sectarian civil war. There is considerable evidence to back these claims. While casualty figures from Iraq have dubious accuracy—a 2008 survey of available data revealed a range of between 34,832 and 793,663 from various sources—there is little doubt that Sunni Arab Iraqis killed thousands of Shi'a Arab Iraqis, and vice versa, throughout the 2004–2008 period.[118] Many of these killings were overtly motivated by sectarian animosity. Sunni insurgent leaders, such as Abu Musab al-Zarqawi, leveraged Sunni Arab Iraqi fears of Shi'a and Persian domination to paint Shi'a as dangerous apostates who must be killed.[119] Extremist Shi'a political leaders and militia commanders painted Sunnis as Ba'athist fascists seeking to return the Shi'a to a position of servitude.[120]

As stated earlier in this section, intersectarian violence during the war both reflected and hardened Muslim Arab sectarian identities. Fear led to killing; killing exacerbated fear, which, in turn, led to more killing. Both fear and killing encouraged Arab Iraqis to seek identities that would offer them the most security and stability. Shi'a had a short line of reasoning to travel to arrive at a hardened Shi'a identity; all the pieces were in place. For the Sunnis, the options were less obvious. Very few Sunnis demonstrated overt identification with Sunni political

---

[118] Hannah Fischer, *Iraqi Civilian Death Estimates*, Washington, D.C.: Congressional Research Service, RS22537, August 27, 2008.

[119] Emily Hunt, "Zarqawi's 'Total War' on Iraqi Shiites Exposes a Divide Among Sunni Jihadists," Washington, D.C.: Washington Institute, November 15, 2005.

[120] See, for example, Cockburn, 2008.

groups or social movements.[121] However, many Sunnis joined, actively supported, or passively supported either nationalist insurgent groups, like the 1920 Revolution Brigade and Jaysh al-Islam, or regional sectarian groups, like Ansar al-Sunnah or (more commonly) AQI.

The nationalist groups tended to focus their efforts against the coalition, while AQI split its exertions against the coalition and Shi'a Arabs. Therefore, at the top level of analysis, the Sunnis who sided with nationalist groups tended to hew to a nationalist form of Sunni identity, while those with AQI were probably more susceptible to salafi-jihadi ideology that, in the Iraq context, viewed Shi'a as an apostate threat. However, many Sunnis who sided with AQI did so not because they believed in Zarqawi's stridently pro-Sunni, anti-Shi'a message but because AQI was the strongest insurgent group in the western and northwestern regions or because AQI offered opportunities to pillage the local Sunni communities. Further, zealots within AQI also saw Sunni nationalists, particularly Sufis who constituted a sizable portion of several key nationalist Ba'athist groups, as apostates. Therefore, even the most overtly Sunni insurgent group was, counterintuitively, also anti-Sunni and not clearly representative of any genuine Sunni identity.[122]

AQI's inability to motivate the Sunnis was manifested in the Anbar Awakening.[123] Sunni Anbaris who had suffered at the hands of both the coalition and AQI eventually decided to rise up against AQI and assist the coalition in securing western Iraq. The Awakening, commonly referred to as the Sunni Awakening, harkened back to the 1995 Armed Dulaymi Tribe's Sons Movement. Motivations for joining the Awakening were myriad; Sunni, tribal, regional, economic, and other identities and motivations were in play. This movement spread to the center and northwest as SoI and concerned local residents groups

---

[121] This is made evident in election results through 2010, as well as the inability of any Sunni political party to mobilize the Sunni Arab Iraqi population.

[122] Analyses of Sunni motivations for insurgency in Iraq are ongoing. See, for example, Montgomery and McWilliams, 2009, and Sterling Jensen, *Iraqi Narratives of the Anbar Awakening*, London: King's College, thesis, 2014.

[123] See, for example, Montgomery and McWilliams, 2009.

formed to defend against various insurgent and militia groups. After Maliki began to erode the Sunni militias, the insurgent movements sprang back to life. Two groups, one nationalist and one salafi-jihadi, would emerge from the eventual, slow-rolling ruin of the Awakening. The first, Jaysh al-Rijal al-Tariqiyeh al-Naqshibandieh was a Sufi Sunni nationalist group led by former Ba'athist military officers. The other was the Islamic State in Iraq, which later evolved into IS.

As the Iraqi Army's politically appointed Shi'a leaders wavered or failed in the face of the IS onslaught in 2014, intensely sectarian Shi'a militias stepped in to fill the gap.[124] These militias, including Sadr's Mahdi Militia, also morphed, endured, and expanded. Sadr now leads the Peace Brigades and the Promised Day Brigades, while the Badr Corps and Asa'ib Ahi al-Haq have grown in both size and strength with the help of the Iranian Revolutionary Guard Corps's Quds Force.[125] As of mid-2015, the Iraqi government had become dependent on the Shi'a militias to not only secure major urban areas but also conduct counter-IS offensive operations. Both militias are increasingly open about their links to Iran, their reverence for the Supreme Leader, and their hatred for Sunni Arabs. The power and influence of Shi'a militias and their overt connection to Iran have both drawn in tens of thousands of Shi'a recruits and terrified the Sunni Arabs. For the time being, at least, IS has co-opted the Sunni narrative, and Iran-backed militias have co-opted the Shi'a narrative. Mid-2015 represented a new high—or low—in intersectarian relations in Iraq.

Implications of Sectarian Division for the Iraqi State and the Region

Hardening sectarian identities among Muslim Arab Iraqis *seemed*, in mid-2015, to be the harbinger of state devolution. Many analysts

---

[124] See, for example, Matt Bradley and Ghassan Adnan, "Shiite Militias Win Bloody Battles in Iraq, Show No Mercy," *Wall Street Journal*, December 5, 2014.

[125] See, for example, C. J. Chivers, "Answering a Cleric's Call, Iraqi Shiites Take Up Arms," *New York Times*, June 21, 2014.

already assume that Kurdish independence is a "when, not if" proposition.[126] Southern and eastern Iraq appear at least on the surface to be monolithic, Iranian-backed Shi'a cantonments supporting aggressive militia-driven land grabs in formerly mixed areas like northern Babil Province and Diyala. Western and northwestern Iraq appear to harbor an intransigent, Gulf Arab–backed, Ba'athist-driven, Sunni minority who either actively or passively support IS. Putting aside the short-sightedness of this monochromatic viewpoint and the myriad other identities and drivers of behavior that are relevant to the current problem, it is necessary to explore the federal option and the possibility of breaking Iraq completely into three separate regions.

Federalism is attractive because it appears to both accept a given ethno-sectarian reality and correct an egregious Western imperialist error: the fabrication of a supposedly impossible Iraqi state. Certainly the vitriol and violence mid-2015 made it difficult to imagine an alternative. Some steps have already been taken toward federal devolution, including the passage of the 2008 Provisional Powers Act. By formalizing the existing federal segregation while retaining the benefits of a central government, Iraq might be able to find naturally occurring stability. Unfortunately, the federal option is unrealistic. Announcement of a federalist policy would immediately accelerate ethno-sectarian cleansing already under way across the front lines between the Shi'a militias and Iraqi Army, the Kurdish security services, and IS.[127] There would be a race to carve out territory before new federal borders were established. Sunni civilians would be most likely to suffer under these conditions, and this suffering would serve only to elongate and inflame the ongoing Sunni revolt against the state.

Once the accelerated cleansing was accomplished, the Sunnis would find themselves with minimal representation in the central government, no economic resources to speak of, damaged cities, and, in

---

[126] See, for example, Zalmay Khalilzad, "Get Ready for Kurdish Independence," *New York Times*, July 13, 2014.

[127] Forecasting analyses in this section represent the informed expert opinions of the authors.

all likelihood, very little support from the center.[128] Given the past reluctance of the Shi'a-led central government to fund development and reconstruction in Sunni-dominated provinces, it is highly unlikely that central government oil revenue would be distributed to Anbar, Nineweh, Salah al-Din, or even the remaining Sunni parts of Ta'mim and Diyala. Further, there is a good possibility that central oil revenues would plummet. Increasing Kurdish independence through federalism would make Kurdish independence more, not less, likely. At the very least, the Kurds would be loath to share in the revenue from their existing resource-rich areas and from those they have seized during the recent fighting. In the south, there is an equally good chance that Basra would seek to negotiate not only increased independence but perhaps even provincial devolution. Basrawi leaders would almost certainly seek to retain greater control over the province's significant oil income. Federalism would exacerbate, not solve, Iraq's problems.

Splitting Iraq along sectarian lines and creating new independent Kurdish, Sunni, and Shi'a states—the complete dissolution of Iraq as a nation—is equally problematic. While some Sunnis have argued for greater federal authority, there is not even a perceptible minority of Sunnis who seek the destruction of the Iraqi state. Instead, driven by cultural expectations and a general belief that population estimates grossly understate Sunni representation, many Sunnis seek to regain control of the state. Nationalism, not devolution or antinationalist revolt, is the primary driver behind Sunni Arab opposition. Similarly, there are no indications that a sizable minority of Shi'a seek the complete disintegration of Iraq. Only Kurdish leaders have expressed an interest in leaving the state, but even these aspirations have been blunted by security fears and by unexpected economic challenges.[129]

---

[128] There is ongoing debate as to how much oil and natural gas exists in the ground in Anbar Province and other Sunni-dominated provinces. Extracting resources in these areas will take considerable time and investment, even if they are sufficient to sustain an independent or semi-independent state. See, for example, John Leland and Khalid D. Ali, "Anbar Province, Once a Hotbed of Iraqi Insurgency, Demands a Say on Resources," *New York Times*, October 27, 2010.

[129] See, for example, Isabel Coles, "Iraq Chaos Fuels Kurds' Independence Dream, but Hurdles Remain," Reuters, July 6, 2014.

There is also no practical way to split Baghdad or the areas around the capital without forcing extraordinary ethnic violence. Deconstructing Iraq would lead to equally artificial borders that would create problems as egregious as—if not more so than—the reviled Sykes-Picot and Anglo-Iraqi accords.

Hardening sectarian identities in Iraq pose a serious problem for the region and for external powers drawn into regional geopolitical rivalries. Because external perception of Iraqi identity is most often simplistic and reductionist, the Saudis, Iranians, and other major regional powers are all quick to view extreme intersectarian violence in Iraq as a clear indicator that Iraq is the epicenter of a regional Sunni-Shi'a war. Western governments seeking a rapid end to the conflict are also quick to define the problem in the simplest terms (as they did in 2003), ignoring centuries of Iraqi history and the complexities of identity that Fanar Haddad, Visser, and other scholars of Iraq believe should receive thoughtful consideration. Just as intersectarian violence has created a fear-kill-fear loop inside Iraq, it has also fed a similar loop across the Middle East. Sunni states see a unified mass of Shi'a across Iran, Iraq, Syria, and Lebanon and attempt to counter Shi'a influence by funding salafi-jihadi extremist groups. These groups then reinforce Shi'a fears of Sunni hegemony and violence. Iran supports the introduction of Lebanese Hezbollah into Iraq, and some Sunnis appear to go as far as to fund IS because it seems like the least bad option in Iraq. As long as Iraq is destabilized, these two fear-kill-fear loops—external and internal—are likely to continue to turn and feed each other for some time.

Possibilities for the Future

There are counternarratives to the notion of a Manichean sectarian divide in Iraq. Fanar Haddad, 2011, offers a different lens through which to view Iraqi identity. He sees identities as coexistent, diffuse, and varying in intensity over time. Through this lens, a Sunni in Ramadi, Anbar Province, Iraq, might identify as a Sunni, with the Sufi subsect; as an Anbari; as a Ramadian; as a tribal confederation member; as a tribal member, as a part-time insurgent group member, as a subtribal member; as a former military officer; as a professional; as a politician; as a parent, brother, sister, son, or daughter; and as a nationalist all at the same time.[130] Because these identities coexist in one Iraqi, they merge and accrue meaning from each other. Nationalism becomes Sunni nationalism, or perhaps Sunni Anbari nationalism. Similarly, a Shi'a from Sadr City might identify as a Shi'a; as an Imami Shi'a; with her city, block, tribe, family, political party, and business council; and as a nationalist. In 2015, sectarian identity was the most obvious Iraqi identity, but it is not the only Iraqi identity. This gives at least faint hope for a postsectarian détente, and perhaps lasting reconciliation and reunification.

There are also practical examples of cross-sectarian relationships during even some of the most-extreme moments of intersectarian violence. Sunni Tarek al-Hashemi's Iraqiyya Party, although it eventually failed and although Hashemi was expelled from Iraq by al-Maliki, was cosectarian. Shi'a Ayad Alawi may not have proven to be the most dynamic or successful leader of Iraq, but his staying power and his acceptance by Sunni Iraqis is remarkable in an era of stark sectarian divisions. The Sunni-led Board of Tribes and Notables of Iraq, a virtual conglomerate of senior Iraqi tribal figures, is constituted of 50-percent Sunni and 50-percent Shi'a membership.[131] Despite years of on-again, off-again ethno-sectarian cleansing, many Sunnis and Shi'a remain closely related by marriage and by tribe. Both the Dulaymi and Shammar confederations cross the sectarian divide. As of early 2016, some Iraqi Arab Sunni internally displaced persons (IDPs) are living in Shi'a areas, primarily in Shi'a homes or Hussayniyah lodgings normally reserved for Shi'a pilgrims. While armed Shi'a groups have reportedly conducted ethnic cleansing of Sunni areas, such as Jurf al-Sakhr, and stopped Sunni IDPs from crossing into safe zones in Fallujat-al-Amariyah, perhaps thousands of Sunni IDPs are reported

---

[130] For a detailed analysis of this argument in the context of military intelligence analysis, see Ben Connable, *Military Intelligence Fusion for Complex Operations*, Santa Monica, Calif.: RAND Corporation, OP-377-RC, 2012.

[131] This group is led by Majed Abed al-Razzaq al-Ali Suleiman al-Dulaymi.

to be living generally safe lives in Shi'a homes and Hussayniyahs across southern Iraq.[132]

If given genuine security and stability, there is little doubt that average Sunnis and average Shi'a would again begin to commingle at the grassroots level. Recent interviews conducted with Sunni Iraqi tribal elders, former military officers, and members of the business community revealed not only a strong sense of nationalism but also a surprisingly strong belief in cosectarian nationalism. While it may have been difficult to envision a unified ethno-sectarian Iraq in mid-2015, envisioning alternative possibilities to ongoing chaos, federalism, or state deconstruction is an important step in moving past the surface-level interpretation of Iraqi identity that continues to hinder both Iraqi and international decisionmaking.

Because the Shi'a now dominate the state almost completely, and because the Sunnis are so badly fragmented and disorganized, it would be incumbent upon the Shi'a leadership to take the first genuine step toward national reconciliation. Sunnis articulated their grievances far more clearly in 2015 than they had during the U.S.-led occupation.[133] Negotiations for reconciliation are probably not possible because there are no Sunni politicians who represent a sizable majority of Iraqis. Therefore, a Shi'a reconciliation package will have to be effected through a massive and convincing fait accompli. This will involve the release of prisoners, extensive funding for reconstruction, and a withdrawal of both Iraqi Army and Shi'a militia forces from Sunni areas. IS's presence will greatly complicate these options, but, if they are properly timed, the Sunnis will help to eject the group from Iraq or to return it to post-2008 dormancy. Genuine hope of reconciliation grounded in state-level legal and economic changes, not payoffs to Sunni elites, is the only reasonable pathway to the second Awakening called for by many Western analysts. Concurrently, the poorly written Iraqi constitution will have to be recrafted to ensure genuine minority protections, to eliminate opportunities for the government to leverage

---

[132] This 2016 assessment is drawn from discussions with senior Iraqi political leaders and Shi'a political leaders in Baghdad, Iraq, in mid-March 2016.

[133] Connable, 2014.

anti-Ba'athism laws against the Sunnis, and to more effectively and realistically address power differentials across the sects and ethnicities in Iraq. This process will give both old and new Sunni politicians a chance to come to the fore in an effort to establish genuine minority rights for Sunnis.

IS is not the greatest hurdle to overcome in achieving stability and security in Iraq. Instead, the greatest hurdles are Shi'a reluctance to trust the Sunnis, and Sunnis' reluctance to accept their de facto minority. Both sets of fears are deeply rooted in Iraqi history. They may be insurmountable, but the alternatives to attempting reunification are either equally bad or far worse.

This chapter has shown that, while Iraq suffers from lasting sectarian divisions, there is nothing inherently intractable or immutable about these problems. Sectarianism in Iraq can exist alongside nationalism, regionalism, tribalism, and many other "isms" without necessarily causing the disintegration of the Iraqi state. Lasting, if uncomfortable, heterogeneity is as possible in Iraq as it is in other states. Instead of focusing on sectarianism as a cause of the current problems in Iraq, observers would find it more effective to think about the intensification of sectarian identity as a consequence of decades of ineffective and oppressive governance and external interventions.

Of course, a strong argument can be made that sectarian identity is and will continue to be decisive in Iraqi politics. It seems undeniable that ethno-sectarianism will play a strong and perhaps dominant role in Iraqi politics, at least for the foreseeable future. Nearly two centuries of Sunni oppression of the Shi'a will not soon be forgotten, nor will the intense violence of the 2006–2007 civil war or the more-recent government oppression of the Sunnis. However, the history of sectarianism in Iraq suggests that it is not too late to avert state fragmentation.

Sunni identity in Iraq has little to do with Sunni interpretations of Islam, and Sunnis did not identify primarily along sectarian lines until well into the past decade. This was perhaps also true of Shi'a Iraqis in the early 1800s: There was a point at which the Ottoman government could have included the Shi'a rather than forcing them to self-organize along sectarian lines. In 2015, Prime Minister al-Abadi had publicly acknowledged that government reform is the key to stability and state survival and that reconciling with the Sunnis is central to this effort.

While poor governance and disastrous intervention intensified sectarianism in Iraq, improved governance and less-meddlesome external support might offer a recipe for eventual stability. This may be true in Iraq and in other areas in the Middle East currently riven by sectarian conflict.

CHAPTER FOUR

Sectarianism in Syria

Introduction

The Syrian Civil War, which began in 2011, is likely to persist for the foreseeable future, with very bleak prospects for a political solution. Sectarianism among Sunni, Alawi and other Shi'a, and other minority groups is playing an increasing role in helping ensure that the Syrian conflict will be a protracted one, but it would be simplistic to refer to sectarian identity as the main source of the uprising against Bashar al-Assad or as the sole motivator of continuing violence. How the conflict is perceived—whether based on sectarianism or other factors—will have an important influence on policies the United States formulates and pursues in Syria and the wider region.

The Bashar al-Assad regime, thanks to Russian intervention and increased Iranian support, remains in control of strategic areas critical to its support base—namely, the capital (Damascus), parts of Idlib and Aleppo and the western region along the Mediterranean coast, and contiguous areas connecting the two. Opposition groups have succeeded in confronting government forces in more-rural areas and small towns of the north, south, and east but are themselves beset with disunity and often battle each other for dominance. Complicating matters significantly are the expanding power of Islamist extremist groups, particularly IS and al-Nusra, and the involvement of competing regional powers, as well as the United States and Russia. The toll this is taking on Syria's population of 22 million already reaches catastrophic proportions, with more than 250,000 killed, more than

1 million wounded, and half the population displaced (3 million in neighboring countries).[1]

In this chapter, we argue that, while governments and groups have used sectarianism effectively to bolster support for their own political agendas, it is only one of several factors that underlie the conflict in Syria, although its importance appears to be increasing. These other factors—geography and locale, political exigency, class differences, and tribal loyalties—both feed and are fed by sectarianism in Syria. Moreover, Syria's historical foundations do not necessarily render sectarianism in the conflict self-evident. This has led one scholar to term the Syrian war "semi-sectarian."[2] But the longer the Syrian conflict continues under the influence of these agendas, the greater the likelihood that the parties to the conflict will default to sectarian preferences. This can also be said of Syrian refugees in neighboring countries and across the region, which could increase instability in the region, particularly in Lebanon.

Following an overview of the mix of ethnic and religious groups in modern Syria, the chapter offers a brief history of the various sects and how their positions in society developed under key periods of pre- and postindependence rule. Subsequently, the chapter describes the role of sectarian association in the context of the 2011 uprising against Bashar al-Assad and how that role quickly evolved as other factors were introduced to the conflict. Finally, the chapter identifies a number of implications of the sectarian factor in Syria and the broader region and presents possibilities for the future.

Syria's Religious and Ethnic Composition: Majority Sunni Arab, but Considerable Diversity Exists

Sunnis make up 68.4 percent of Syria's population, with some 13 percent of Sunnis of Kurdish ethnicity and the remainder Arab. Sunni Arabs are spread throughout Syria, as seen in Figure 4.1, while Kurds

---

[1]   See UN News Centre, "News Focus: Syria," undated; and Uri Friedman, "Almost Half of Syria's Population Has Been Uprooted," *Atlantic*, August 2014.

[2]   Christopher Phillips, "Sectarianism and Conflict in Syria," *Third World Quarterly*, Vol. 36, No. 2, March 24, 2015, p. 357.

Figure 4.1
Distribution of Religious and Ethnic Groups in Syria

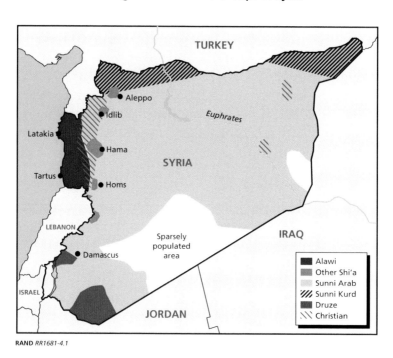

RAND *RR1681-4.1*

reside mostly in the northeast and northwest sections of the country near the Turkish border. The next-largest sects are the Alawis, who constitute 11.3 percent of Syria's population, and Christians, at 11.2 percent. Alawis are concentrated in the western mountain region of Jabal Nusayriyyah along the Mediterranean coast between the Turkish border to the north and the Lebanese border to the south. Christians (mostly Eastern Orthodox) are to the east, between this mountain range and the cities of Idlib, Hama, and Homs; there are also concentrations in the southwest near Damascus and Deraa, as well as to the east near Deir az-Zur and Hasaka. Ismaili and Twelver Shi'a represent about 3.2 percent, as do the Druze. The Shi'a reside primarily near Aleppo, Idlib, Hama, and Homs, while the Druze are in the south along the border with Jordan and to the west abutting the borders of Lebanon and the Israeli-annexed Golan Heights. The remaining 2.6 percent of the population is composed of Circassians, Turkmen, and others.[3] No region is entirely homogeneous, and ethno-religious groups commingle in most areas, or did until the civil war.

While variations among Sunnis and Shi'a are discussed earlier in this report, in Syria's case, it is important to focus on the Alawi community. The Alawis are a sect that has been associated for various reasons with Shi'ism (see next section) but in fact has separate tenets and practices and has been shunned in the past by both Sunnis and Shi'a in part because of its heterodoxy. The Alawi faith originated in the tenth and 11th centuries and adopted pagan, Shi'a, and Christian practices.[4] The sect was founded by Muhammad Ibn Nusayr al-Bakri an-Namiri—Alawis are referred to as "Nusayris," particularly by Sunni salafi or jihadist elements whose intention is derogatory—and took root in the Mediterranean town of Latakia and the surrounding mountain communities. The Jabal Nusayriyyah mountain range served to geographically separate the Alawis from other sects and allowed them to maintain a homogeneous identity until modern times, leading historians to term them, like the Druze in Lebanon, a *compact minority*.[5]

The Role of Sectarian Identity in Syria Prior to the 2011 Revolt

Historically, friction among sects in Syria (and Lebanon) has been driven less by religious or theological differences over Islamic succession or heterodoxy than by other, more "practical" factors. Though religious heterodoxy has appeared periodically as a source of open contention among communities, other factors, including geography and

---

[3]   Michael Izady, "Syria: Religious Composition (Summary)," map, Columbia University Gulf 2000 Project, 2015.

[4]   The Alawis adopted the ideas of a divine triad from paganism, the cult of Ali (Mohammed's cousin and son-in-law) from Shi'ism and mysticism from Ismaili Shi'ism, and the use of ceremonial wine and observance of Christmas from Christianity. See Farouk-Alli, 2014, p. 209.

[5]   A term popularized by historian Albert Hourani, *compact minority* is one that makes up a large proportion of the population in a geographically limited or restricted area. See Farouk-Alli, 2014, p. 210.

locale, political exigency, class differences, and economic inequalities have also driven sects in Syria to draw together in a defensive crouch or to criticize or demonize their opposites. For much of their history until modern times, for example, the Alawis had been a separatist minority sect that often had been economically deprived, geographically isolated, and at times persecuted. When it has arisen in Syrian history, sectarianism has occurred mainly between Alawis and Sunnis and occasionally has involved the Shia, Druze, and Christian communities.

Early Sectarian Identity in Preindependence Syria

While much of the sectarian history of the region is covered earlier in this report, it is important here to note that certain key events in Syria's early history have informed today's sectarian environment. The region of Latakia and its environs remained somewhat insulated from wholesale Islamicization during conversion efforts by various rulers, which allowed the Alawi sect west of Jabal Nusayriyyah to expand over time and to borrow rituals from Shi'ism while maintaining a separate identity. But Alawi-Sunni tension was substantial in the Crusader Wars, during which the Sunnis accused the Alawis (and the Christians) of supporting the Europeans, and persisted into the 14th century, when Sunni salafi scholar Taqi ad-Din Ahmad Ibn Taymiyyah issued a fatwa proclaiming the Nusayris, as he termed them, to be

> more disbelieving than the Jews and the Christians. . . . There is no doubt that fighting these . . . is a great sign of obedience (to God); it is superior to fighting polytheists and "people of the book" [Jews and Christians] who do not fight the Muslims.[6]

Alawi conscription into the army under the Ottomans in the mid–19th century broke the geographic isolation afforded by Jabal Nusayriyyah and "was the first step towards the social transformation and integration of the Alawis into the institutional apparatuses of the

---

[6] Quoted in Nazih Ayubi, *Political Islam: Religion and Politics in the Arab World*, London: Routledge, 1993, pp. 88–89. The role of Ibn Taymiyyah in the jihadist movement today is profound; some portray him as one of the ideological fathers of the Islamic State of Iraq and the Levant.

State and, as such, into the broader social fabric of Syrian society as well."[7] At the same time, Western advancement of political and economic interests in the weakening Ottoman Empire involved championing individual religious communities in Syria. The provision of education (and growing secular nationalism among Arab intelligentsia) awakened the Alawis' desire for integration with the Muslim mainstream and led them to declare themselves as adherents to Shi'a Islam.[8]

However, as stated previously, the French sought during the Mandate for Syria and Lebanon in the 1920s and 1930s to weaken the growing nationalist aspirations of the Sunni majority by sharpening sectarian separatism and fragmentation in Syria.[9] The French elevated the Alawis' economic and political status and offered autonomy but did not succeed in quelling the growing Alawi desire to unite with other communities in a single Syrian state. The 1936 Franco-Syrian Treaty of Independence, along with a fatwa by the Mufti of Palestine that the Alawis should be considered Muslims, paved the way for political and social integration despite some efforts by separatist Alawis to violently resist the Sunni-dominated nationalist government before and after Syrian independence in 1946.[10] By this time, the Sunni Arabs had come to dominate the officer corps in the Syrian Army and controlled the government, while the Alawis were overrepresented among the army's rank-and-file soldiers.[11] The army attracted minorities from disadvantaged backgrounds and provided them with upward economic

---

[7]   Farouk-Alli, 2014, p. 212.

[8]   Farouk-Alli, 2014, p. 213.

[9]   League of Nations, "Mandate for Syria and the Lebanon," London, July 24, 1922. In fact, the French emphasized sectarian differences as an argument for the mandate. See Daniel Neep, *Occupying Syria Under the French Mandate: Insurgency, Space and State Formation*, Cambridge, UK: Cambridge University Press, 2012, p. 26.

[10]   See Eyal Zisser, "The Alawis, Lords of Syria: From Ethnic Minority to Ruling Sect," in Ofra Bengio and Gabriel Ben-Dor, eds., *Minorities and the State in the Arab World*, Boulder, Colo.: Lynne Riener Publishers, 1999, pp. 131–133; and Farouk-Alli, 2014, pp. 213–216.

[11]   Ayse Tekdal Fildis, "Roots of Alawite-Sunni Rivalry in Syria," *Middle East Policy Council*, Vol. 19, No. 2, Summer 2012.

and social mobility; at the same time, Sunni urban elites avoided rank-and-file service, seeing it as "socially undistinguished."[12]

The societal integration among the sects that evolved under the banner of nationalism in preindependence Syria helped pave the way for a unified republic. But it did not erase centuries of marginalization of the Alawis or Sunni resentment of Alawis as socially inferior and undeserving of advancement. This would lay the foundation for latent sectarian tension under the al-Assad regimes.

Sectarian Identity in Modern Syria: From Independence Through the Rule of Hafez al-Assad

The decade following Syrian independence in 1946 was a time of political instability and uncertainty as multiple coups brought down a succession of governments in Damascus. Two important movements were established in Syria—the Muslim Brotherhood and the Ba'ath Party—that had an important bearing on the political and sectarian development of the country. The Brotherhood, originally established in Egypt in 1928, arose in Syria during the 1930s as a social movement. Its orientation was, and remains, sectarian and Sunni Islamist and would later bring it into conflict with the regime of Hafez al-Assad. In contrast, the Ba'ath Party—founded by a Christian named Michel Aflag—took root in both Syria and Iraq in the 1940s with a focus on secularism and socialism. The party was instrumental to the Alawis' later ascension to power in Syria (though less so than the army was) because of its nondiscriminatory agenda that attracted minority communities. The party expanded quickly in the Latakia region and served as a means of incorporation of the increasingly educated Alawis into the Syrian polity. By the time of the Ba'athist overthrow of the government in 1963, Alawis and other minorities had joined Sunnis in reaching the officer corps in the army and the upper echelons of the Ba'ath Party and had become largely integrated into society. At the same time, an urban elite and middle class had emerged, consisting largely of Sunnis

---

[12] Farouk-Alli, 2014, p. 217.

but also including these minorities. This was a time of relative sectarian comity in Syria.[13]

After a period of instability under the Ba'athist government, one of these Alawi officers, Hafez al-Assad, took power in 1970. His rule until his death in 2000 emphasized anti-imperialism, redistribution of wealth to poorer classes, pan-Arabism, and nostalgia for ancient glory of Arab empires. He sought outwardly to temper sectarian divisions through secularism but also co-opted various sectarian groups and developed patrimonial networks to strengthen his rule. He even embraced Islamic symbolism as a means of attracting Sunni support, including praying in Sunni mosques and making hajj to Mecca like other Muslim leaders in the Middle East. He had Alawis declared Shi'a Muslims under the auspices of an influential Iranian cleric in Lebanon, Ayatollah Musa Sadr, which helped forge common political interests between the Alawis and the regime on one hand and Syria's small Shi'a minority on the other and laid groundwork for a strategic alliance with Iran. All of this helped the secular al-Assad burnish his Islamic credentials, but his use of religion was "no more than a convenient tool for influencing politics."[14]

Hafez al-Assad's secularism and co-option of the various sects in Syria were instrumental to his survival and power by deemphasizing his own status as a minority Alawi while portraying the Alawi sect as mainstream. Still, al-Assad ruled through his own personal constituency. Though he appointed Sunnis to key positions, including his longtime defense minister, Mustafa Tlas, the core membership of the ruling elite extended outwardly from his family, tribe, and Alawi sect. Al-Assad created a *"mukhabarat* state" that involved multiple layers of security apparatus to ensure identification and elimination of internal threats—at times violently. Notably, after three years of internal strife against Islamists described as "close to civil

---

[13]   See Steven Heydemann, *Authoritarianism in Syria: Institutions and Social Conflict 1946–1970*, Ithaca, N.Y.: Cornell University Press, 1999.

[14]   See Farouk-Alli, 2014, p. 219. Al-Assad even had an amendment added to Syria's constitution that mandated that the president must be Muslim, a stipulation put forward in the 1950s by the founder of the Brotherhood's Syrian branch.

war," the Hafez al-Assad government ruthlessly put down a Muslim Brotherhood–inspired uprising in Hama in February 1982, besieging the town for nearly a month and killing an estimated 20,000 people— an event that essentially eliminated the antisecular Brotherhood as a political force in Syria.[15] Until the Hama massacre, al-Assad had risked losing the support of large parts of his constituent base, including public-sector workers and the urban middle class.[16] His son Bashar al-Assad drew lessons from this chapter in Syrian history in his brutal responses to the 2011 uprising.

Internally, the government of Hafez al-Assad maintained his tight grip on power through a number of complex strategies implemented through the Ba'ath Party. While he provided minority groups, including his own Alawi sect, with privileges and access, he also perpetuated secularism while empowering government-sanctioned Sunni clerical networks. Economically, he secured the fortunes of Sunni and Christian merchant classes in return for their loyalty. He used sectarianism to divide and conquer, but under the guise of national unity and secularism. Externally, Hafez al-Assad's focus on pan-Arab causes and resistance to Israel—including support of Shi'a groups, such as Lebanese Hezbollah, and Sunni Islamist Palestinian groups like Hamas and Islamic Jihad—helped attract broad-based support and distracted observers from the fact of minority rule in Syria by emphasizing non-sectarian nationalism. Hafez al-Assad also cemented a close strategic relationship with the Islamic Republic of Iran when the Soviet Union, Syria's long-time patron, dissolved in the early 1990s.[17]

Hafez al-Assad's use of nationalism and secularism was instrumental to maintaining a tight grip on power for 30 years, and large sectors of Syrian society "seemingly bought into the regime and its

---

[15]   Volker Perthes, *The Political Economy of Syria Under Assad*, London: I. B. Taurus and Company, 1997, p. 136.

[16]   Perthes, 1997.

[17]   Emile Hokayem, *Syria's Uprising and the Fracturing of the Levant, Adelphi Series*, Vol. 53, No. 438, June 14, 2013, p. 18. See also Heydemann, 1999.

inclusive nationalist rhetoric."[18] But his power also derived from exploitation of communal interests. His power base had an Alawi core. That community benefited considerably under his rule, both economically and politically, creating in the minds of many Syrians deep resentment and an inextricable linkage to the regime.[19] This privilege and resentment, which increased under Hafez's son Bashar al-Assad, would later sow the seeds for sectarianism during the civil war by rendering anti-Alawi and antiregime narratives by extremist Sunni groups attractive to broader Syrian audiences.

Contemporary Sectarian Identity in Syria Under Bashar al-Assad

Bashar al-Assad continued his father's policies and strategies after the elder's death in 2000 but also adopted liberalizing economic policies that had the effect of disenfranchising the al-Assads' traditional power base among rural populations and the working class while perpetuating and even deepening corruption and "center-periphery inequalities."[20] It was frustration with the Syrian government's clientelism and inability to provide basic services in the periphery—not sectarian tension or animosity—that helped fuel the initial protests of March 2011.

But Bashar's actions in the decade prior to the revolt also encouraged an environment in which sectarianism could be more easily exploited to support political and ideological agendas once public order devolved into open conflict. To consolidate his power, Bashar removed Sunni stalwarts of his father's administration in 2005 in favor of members of the al-Assad family, thereby increasing Alawi domination of the regime. Second, Bashar's economic policies enriched a new, Alawi-dominated elite that flaunted its wealth and "became a visible symbol

---

[18] Phillips, 2015, p. 366. For more on how al-Assad co-opted large sectors of Syrian society through the use of secularism and nationalism, see Perthes, 1997; and Hanna Batutu, *Syria's Peasantry, The Descendants of Its Lesser Rural Notables, and Their Politics*, Princeton, N.J.: Princeton University Press, 1999.

[19] Farouk-Alli, 2014, p. 220.

[20] Benedetta Berti and Jonathan Paris, "Beyond Sectarianism: Geopolitics, Fragmentation, and the Syrian Civil War," *Strategic Assessment*, Vol. 16, No. 4, January 2014, pp. 22–23. See also Bassam Haddad, *Business Networks in Syria: The Political Economy of Authoritarian Resilience*, Stanford, Calif.: Stanford University Press, 2012.

of regime excess" and increased animosity and jealousy among other sects, which began to resent the Alawis for their economic and political entitlements.[21] This helped inextricably tie the Alawi community to the al-Assad regime. Third, social and other services at the local level were increasingly abandoned by the government and taken up by nonstate groups defined by religion or sect. Finally, Bashar's Iraq policy, aimed at weakening the U.S. occupation of and interests in Iraq by facilitating the transit of jihadist fighters, opened the door for a return of those fighters to Syria and the spread of their extremist ideologies.[22]

While sectarianism did not appear outwardly in Bashar's first decade of rule, one anthropologist's fieldwork in Syria in the 1990s corroborated the reemergence of sectarian affiliation not based on religion or heterodoxy but on a combination of communal interest, class, and region.[23] Noting that the once-downtrodden Alawis experienced "a stunning reversal of fortune within living memory" that displaced traditional urban elites (largely Sunni but only by affiliation), she writes that "each group assumes the other's advantage: Alawis point to the enduring prosperity of Damascus' [Sunni] 'merchant princes;' [Sunni] Damascenes to well-placed Alawis' control of licensing and smuggling."[24] Thus, while sectarian animosity was not a primary feature of Syrian society under Bashar, its existence as an undercurrent allowed it to bubble to the surface when political factors triggered the breakdown of civil–government relations.

Sectarianism in Syria Following the 2011 Revolt

The uprising against the Bashar al-Assad regime began as a non- (or cross-) sectarian revolt against authoritarian rule, corruption, social inequality, and bad governance. Mobilization of various internal

---

[21] Phillips, 2015, p. 367.

[22] Phillips, 2015, pp. 366–368.

[23] See Christa Salamandra, "Sectarianism in Syria: Anthropological Reflections," *Middle East Critique*, Vol. 22, No. 3, 2013, pp. 303–306.

[24] Salamandra, 2013, p. 305.

groups was based more on where members lived and their relationship with the government than on religious affiliation. This is particularly the case given that the uprising began in the southern Syrian town of Deraa, a poor agricultural region of mixed sects that suffered the loss of government services under al-Assad's economic policies.[25] While the revolt was indeed overwhelmingly Sunni, it was communal resentment rather than ideological or sectarian motivation that sparked it. It is important to note that, at times, al-Assad has turned his guns on his own sect: The Syrian navy shelled the predominantly Alawi "capital" city of Latakia in response to antigovernment demonstrations in August 2011.[26] Similarly, IS is known for combating rival Sunni armed groups—including so-called jihadists—as much as Shi'a and other non-Sunni armed elements.

However, the conflict quickly took on sectarian overtones due to the Bashar al-Assad government's response, the involvement of external regional actors with conflicting political agendas, and the expanded participation of extremist groups as major combatants in the Syria arena. Actions on both sides have raised the enmity of Sunnis and Alawis against each other for communitarian, not theological, reasons. Graham Fuller suggests that

> The problem is that if we view these conflicts through primarily religious lenses we are indeed accepting them as "primordial" conflicts, that is, never really susceptible to rational solution. But to view them as power struggles, rival interests, at least reduces the problem to issues of changeable conditions of political governance. It is astonishing how quickly sectarian differences can vanish again under conditions of social order and prosperity, when members of both communities have other interests to absorb their attention than simply pursuing sectarian rivalries. But right now we don't at all have conditions of social order and prosperity; the destruction of Iraq in the US invasion, and the

---

[25]   See Joshua Landis, "The Syrian Uprising of 2011: Why the Asad Regime Is Likely to Survive to 2013," *Middle East Policy Council*, Vol. XIX, No. 1, Spring 2012, p. 6.

[26]   Michael J. Totten, "Assad Shells Alawite Stronghold," *World Affairs Journal*, August 13, 2011.

subsequent internal war in Syria, have both produced optimal conditions for today's sectarian hatreds in their most emotional and violent form.[27]

The complexity of the Syrian Civil War is demonstrated in the approach to and behavior of some tribes in the Raqqa region, now controlled by IS. Traditional tribal elites, who tend to outwardly support the strongest party to ensure that the tribe can avoid violence and repression, are important sources of local mobilization. Prior to the 2011 uprising, for example, the Sunni al-Bariyaj clan of the al-'Afadla tribe was considered the Bashar al-Assad government's closest ally in Raqqa. In the immediate aftermath of the uprising, al-Assad enlisted al-Bariyaj fighters as *shabiha* militia—a paramilitary force of regime loyalists (mostly Alawis in other parts of the country) created to violently suppress demonstrations and attack antiregime activists. Yet when IS became the dominant power there, the clan was actively courted by and transferred allegiance to IS and, in mid-2014, provided an important segment of local fighters for the group. Sectarianism has little to do with tribal loyalties that derive from the complicated but more-pragmatic motivations of self-protection and local rivalries.[28]

Sectarian identity is being exploited by several key parties to the conflict to ensure support of constituencies and instill fear, while the most-extreme elements on both sides "are inherently motivated by sectarian animus" as a matter of ideology.[29] There are Alawi and other minority groups who oppose the Bashar al-Assad government and Sunnis who have thrown their lot in with it—for reasons of political belief or economic well-being. Clearly, then, the conflict is not divided neatly along sectarian lines.

---

[27] Graham E. Fuller, "Why Does ISIS Hate Shi'a?" lobelog.com, December 17, 2014.

[28] Felix Legrand, "The Colonial Strategy of ISIS in Syria," *Arab Reform Initiative: Policy Alternatives*, June 2014, p. 6.

[29] M. Zuhdi Jasser, "Sectarian Conflict in Syria," *PRISM*, Vol. 4: *Syria Supplemental*, Center for Complex Operations, National Defense University, 2014, p. 60.

The Bashar al-Assad Government Has Fueled Sectarian Tension to Ensure Survival

The government response to peaceful protests in 2011 was a violent one that not only forced the opposition to take up arms, but also brought out sectarian identity as a factor in the conflict. The al-Assad regime—whose ultimate goal is survival—has sought to magnify sectarian fears among Alawis and Shi'a to maintain a strong constituency and among Christians and Druze to maintain their neutrality if not gain their support. The regime has enlisted Iran's military, political, and financial support,[30] which has in turn recruited external Shi'a militias using anti-Sunni rhetoric and calls to defend Shi'a holy sites in Syria (see the section later in this chapter on external actors).

Early on, the regime employed sectarian rhetoric as a means of perpetuating an image of embattled minorities whose well-being depended upon unity with the government and of opposing forces that were Islamist extremists supported by foreign backers. Soon after the initial protests, Syrian state media began referring to demonstrators (who were predominantly Sunni but in fact hailed from all sects) as sectarian Islamists. *Shabiha* were used to deliver sandbags to Alawi villages under the guise of protecting them from rampaging Sunnis nearby but with the real intention of instilling fear in the Alawi community. Later, as battlefield losses prompted the regime to enlist external sectarian actors like Hezbollah and Iraqi Shi'a militias, it also began creating sect-based local defense units among Druze, Christians, and Alawis and allowed the public appearance of sect-based symbols (such as the Druze star and the Shi'a sword) alongside national symbols—something forbidden prior to the revolt.[31]

The 2013 battle for the town of al-Qusayr in a mixed Sunni-Shi'a area near the border with northeast Lebanon was an important turning point that exacerbated the sectarian vector of the conflict. Lebanese Hezbollah forces assaulted surrounding Sunni villages and, in combination with Syrian Army units, took the town from Sunni rebels in

---

[30] See Mohsen Milani, "Why Tehran Won't Abandon Assad(ism)," *Washington Quarterly*, Vol. 36, No. 4, Spring 2013, pp. 79–93.

[31] Phillips, 2015, p. 369.

June. In strategic terms, this could be seen as an effort by the Bashar al-Assad regime to strengthen lines of communication for support from Lebanese territory. However, the entry of the prominent Shi'a militant group into the Syrian Civil War in support of the regime also served to emphasize some of the sectarian nature of support for al-Assad and intensify Sunni sectarian rhetoric, particularly from external sources.[32]

The regime commonly refers to the Sunni Arab–dominated opposition as *takfiris* who present a severe threat to Syria's ethnic and religious minorities.[33] Al-Assad himself has been quoted frequently making this case, for example in a meeting with the Syriac Orthodox Church, where he is reported to have said that "the terrorist aggression against the region and the *takfiri* extremist mentality underlying it target the diverse social and cultural fabric of the region in general and Syria in particular."[34] It makes little distinction between Sunni extremists in the opposition, such as IS and al-Nusra, and more-moderate elements in the FSA or the National Coalition, referring to them all as "terrorists" and emphasizing their Sunni nature. In a 2013 interview with *Le Figaro*, al-Assad commented, "We are fighting terrorists. . . . 80–90 percent belong to al-Qaeda. They are not interested in reform or in politics. The only way to deal with them is to annihilate them."[35]

The regime has sought to magnify the sectarian nature of violence perpetrated by the opposition, emphasizing its brutality as a means of reinforcing fears among Alawis, Christians, and other minorities that they cannot live safely under a Sunni-dominated government in Syria.[36] State media widely report cases of sectarian cleansing by mili-

---

[32] See Steven Heydemann, "Syria's Uprising: Sectarianism, Regionalisation, and State Order in the Levant," Fundación para las Relaciones Internacionales y el Diálogo Exterior working paper 119, May 2013; and Aaron Reese, "Sectarian and Regional Conflict in the Middle East," Middle East Security Report 13, Institute for the Study of War, July 2013.

[33] A *takfiri* is a Muslim who accuses other Muslims of being apostates and deserving of death (Philip Smyth, *The Shiite Jihad in Syria and its Regional Effects*, Washington Institute for Near East Policy, Policy Focus 138, 2015).

[34] "Assad: Takfiri Terrorism Targets Diverse Social, Cultural Fabric of Region," Syrian Arab News Agency, June 11, 2015.

[35] Quoted in Berti and Paris, 2014, p. 24.

[36] Smyth, 2015, pp. 8–12.

tant Islamist groups, while "car bombings, including a massive explosion in the Alawi district of Mezze 86 in Damascus in November 2012, seemed to justify the fear of an impending jihadi slaughter" of what the extremists viewed as Alawi heretics.[37] At the same time, the regime has portrayed itself as a protector of religious moderation and stability to appeal to "the multi-confessional urban middle class and the large number of bureaucrats and public sector employees whose status and benefits depended on the regime."[38] This message was attractive to that audience, which justifiably felt threatened by the rise and influence of jihadist groups advocating Islamic law and oppression of minorities. The regime's strategy has been to combine divisiveness based on communal identity with inclusiveness and nationalism depending on the targeted constituency. Bashar al-Assad has sought to walk a fine line between raising the mantle of security, counterterrorism, and nationalism to appeal to broad domestic constituencies and international (especially Western) audiences on one hand, and stoking fears of sectarian persecution to draw in minority communities in Syria and external actors like Iran and Hezbollah on the other.

Sunni Anti-Alawi and Anti-Shi'a Sectarianism in Syria Has Grown

As radical Sunni jihadist groups have emerged as a more dominant force among the opposition both on the battlefield and in the public eye, so too has a more strident form of sectarianism. The ideologies of these groups are fundamentally based on an essentialist worldview and the vehement rejection of heterodoxy as they define it. Anti-Shi'a and anti-Alawi (or anti-Nusayri) rhetoric—as well as ideology and violent action—is particularly virulent from IS, while strong but somewhat more moderate from the al-Qaeda–affiliated al-Nusra. Sectarianism has also appeared in areas it has held for a period of time where the areas must administer services to populations under their control.

IS habitually refers to Shi'a as *rawafidh*, or rejectionists, who are infidels and reject the true Islam, and to Alawis as *Nusayri* in a manner

---

[37]   Hokayem, 2013, p. 53.

[38]   Hokayem, 2013, p. 54.

meant to be derogatory. In a March 2015 video produced by its Hama Province Media Office, an IS representative exclaimed that

> "The *rafidhi* [Shi'a] is an impure disbeliever." Allah the most exalted said: "So when you meet (in fight—jihad in Allah's cause) those who disbelieve, smite (their) necks." . . . We will not forget what happened in the 1980s, or what the immoral Nusayri regime did to the Muslims in Hama. We will not forget every single drop of Muslim blood that was shed on that blessed land. It is the same as the Caliph said: "So by Allah, we will take revenge! By Allah, we will take revenge! Even if it takes a while, every amount of harm will be responded to with multitudes more."[39]

While its ideology and rhetoric are vehemently anti-Shi'a, IS has mostly fought other Sunni-dominated opposition groups in Syria—an important distinction from its pursuits in Iraq. This may derive from the group's dedication to gaining control of territory to establish a caliphate, a pursuit that pits it against other Sunni groups in areas where the regime has ceded territory. Moreover, it is important to note that IS does not have a state patron and has been largely self-funded. While some wealthy individuals in the Gulf states have provided monetary contributions and volunteers have come from these countries to fight under IS, there is no evidence of direct support from the Saudi or Qatari governments, and, in fact, they see IS as a threat to their own interests. Thus, the virulent sectarian rhetoric and actions taken by IS should not be seen fundamentally as originating externally.[40]

In its governance of Syrian areas under its control, IS has instituted a pact with minorities who were unable or chose not to flee as its fighters defeated regime forces and rival groups in eastern Syria—a decidedly political decision by a highly ideological group as a means of ruling a diverse ethno-religious population. This pact levies a special tax (*jizya*) on remaining Christians in Raqqa and prohibits them

---

[39] "Smite Their Necks," video, SITE translation, Hama Province Islamic State, March 28, 2015.

[40] Gause, 2014. Much of the funding for IS has come from oil sales, extortion, and smuggling.

from displaying religious symbols in public, repairing or building new churches, or in any way disparaging Islam. The *jizya* was traditionally levied on Christian and Jewish citizens under the early Muslim caliphs because they had special status as "people of the Book" (*ahl al-dhimmi*). These people were considered second-class citizens but had certain rights protected under sharia law. But rather than serving to protect minorities as the pact had been intended under the caliphs, IS uses it as a form of disenfranchisement.[41]

Al-Nusra's sectarian rhetoric is somewhat toned down from that of IS, leaving it somewhat more open to temporary alliances of convenience with less sectarian Sunni opposition groups, though it remains strongly sectarian in ideology and rhetoric. It refers to Alawis by the derogatory *Nusayri* (except in interviews with foreign media), and calls Shi'a *rawafidh* less frequently than does IS. But its communiqués continue to state that killing *rawafidh* (Shi'a) is obligatory, chastises IS for not killing enough of them, and even draws parallels between Shi'a and IS in its competition with that group. Accusing IS of "betrayal, treachery, and lies," al-Nusra states that "this is a quality that resembles the qualities of the *rawafidh*."[42]

In an interview with *Al Jazeera* in May 2015, al-Nusra emir Abu-Muhammad al-Julani stated that Alawis would be accepted only if they converted to al-Nusra's brand of Islam, commenting that "Alawis who turn their backs on the regime, repent, and embrace Islam will be regarded as brothers and will be forgiven."[43] Alawis are thereby given a choice of conversion or death. In the same interview, al-Julani offers Christians a more lenient choice because, while many of them support the Bashar al-Assad regime, "we are not at war with them." He goes on to offer that, "if the Christians repent, they will be succumbed to Shari'a laws and will pay *jizya*," or tax levied upon *ahl al-dhimmi*. Thus,

---

[41]   Charles C. Caris and Samuel Reynolds, *ISIS Governance in Syria*, Middle East Security Report 22, Institute for the Study of War, July 2014, p. 16.

[42]   Al-Nusra, "The Group of 'Dawlah'—and the Islamic Ruling Regarding It," SITE translation, March 5, 2015a.

[43]   Pieter Van Ostaeyan, "Al-Jazeera: Interview with Jabhat al-Nusra Amir Abu-Muhammad al-Julani," blog post, translation, May 27, 2015.

al-Nusra would demand conversion from Alawis but not from Christians. In areas it controls, al-Nusra appears to be providing food, electricity and water, and health care, in one town "provided from a small clinic that treats all comers, regardless of whether they have sworn allegiance to the emirate or not."[44] However, while the differences between the competing IS and al-Nusra may leave the latter more amenable to working with other opposition groups, both remain highly sectarian in terms of rhetoric, ideology, and actions.

External Actors Have Exacerbated Sectarianism in Syria

The power struggle between Saudi Arabia and Iran and their respective "blocs" in the Syrian conflict is less an originating factor in the uprising and more a catalyst that exploits and fans the increasingly sectarian nature of the conflict in the context of the two countries' own geostrategic competition. Sunni Saudi Arabia and Shi'a Iran vie for regional prominence and influence, seek to preserve their own antithetical political systems, and lay opposing claims to leadership of the Muslim world. While this competition for influence is covered in greater depth in Chapter Six, it has a strong bearing on sectarianism in the Syrian conflict. Saudi and Iranian provision of resources and support to opposing forces in Syria, in combination with calls for Sunni or Shi'a jihad against the other from clerics on both sides, provides fertile ground for reinforcing sectarian trends in the conflict.

Besides providing the Bashar al-Assad government military materiel, training, and advice, Tehran has orchestrated an influx of foreign militias and fighters into Syria to shore up the regime. This effort became urgent in 2012 as battlefield losses by Syrian government forces increasingly threatened the survival of Iran's close ally in Damascus.[45] Lebanese Hezbollah offered its fighters and its considerable battlefield experience to help reinforce key lines of communication in Syria and reverse government territorial losses in strategically crucial areas. Hez-

---

[44] Geith Abdul-Ahad, "Syria's al-Nusra Front—Ruthless, Organised and Taking Control," *Guardian*, July 10, 2013.

[45] Luke Harding, Miriam Elder, and Peter Beaumont, "Assad Losing Syria War, Russia Admits for First Time," *Guardian*, December 13, 2012.

bollah's motivation was, first and foremost, a deep concern that it could lose a strong ally in Damascus and its primary conduit for arms and other support from Tehran. It has also waded into the sectarian divide. But it has had to be quite cautious because of its position in Lebanon as part of the government and where an overt sectarian approach to the war would exacerbate existing tensions with other, particularly Sunni, sectors of the Lebanese population.

More broadly, however, Tehran has appealed to other foreign fighters and groups to pursue a Shi'a jihad to defend their fellow Shi'a and the holy places, drawing them into the Syrian Civil War on Bashar al-Assad's side. Multiple Shi'a militia organizations have appeared in Syria composed of fighters from Lebanon, Iraq, Pakistan, and even Afghanistan, attracted by their shared willingness to combat *takfiri* jihadists and protect their coreligionists.

A central factor drawing outside Shi'a groups has been defense of the sacred, gold-domed shrine of Sayyida Zainab, sister of the martyred third Shi'a imam al-Hussein Ibn Ali Ibn Abi Talib, located just south of Damascus. The mantra *"Labayk ya Zainab!"* (At your service, O Zainab!) has been chanted at funerals of Lebanese and Iraqi fighters killed in Syria, and the shrine's distinct gold dome is prominent in Shi'a martyrdom posters.[46] One of the more-prominent militant Shi'a groups in Syria, Liwa Abu Fadl al-Abbas, claimed in its first official statement in June 2013 that its only goal was to "defend holy sites in Syria."[47] As the war has drawn on, a form of "pan-Shi'ism" has emerged in which Shi'a militant groups, as well as Iran itself, claim to protect not only sacred sites but also the Shi'a community writ large.[48]

In terms of demonizing the opposition, Iran and Shi'a groups such as Hezbollah have cast the opposition as *takfiris*.[49] Such expres-

---

[46] Smyth, 2015, pp. 3–4.

[47] Smyth, 2015, Appendix 2, p. 2.

[48] Smyth, 2015, pp. 7–8.

[49] Hezbollah's official news outlet, al-Manar, provides multiple examples of this language. See, for example, "Takfiri Terrorists Commit Massacre Against Syrian Druze in Idleb Countryside," *al-Manar*, June 11, 2015; and "Hezbollah, Syrian Army Advance in Jarajir Barrens," *al-Manar*, June 12, 2015.

sions have been underwritten by Iran's Supreme Leader, who, while not issuing a public fatwa on the war, has reportedly encouraged subordinate clerics to issue their own fatwas justifying jihad in Syria and issued religious obligations (*taqlif sharii*) to Shi'a militant groups to join the fight. Failure to heed these obligations is seen as the equivalent of disobeying the word of God.[50]

External Sunni actors—which include not only Saudi Arabia but Qatar and Turkey, as well as individual clerics—also have couched some of their support of Syrian opposition groups and motivations for defeating the Bashar al-Assad government in sectarian terms, although not uniformly. Turkey had allowed foreign fighters to cross into Syria during the initial uprising against al-Assad and has only recently sought to systematically crack down on these movements.[51] Turkey has also sought to protect the small Syrian Turkman minority of about 200,000, considered ethnic kin, and has supported Turkman militias.[52] The Saudis have sought to exploit sectarianism in Syria to bring down Iran's ally in Damascus yet initially supported the least sectarian of the rebel groups in Syria, the FSA, and other anti–al-Assad groups in Syria that shunned alliance with the Muslim Brotherhood, which has competed with the Saudis in the past. They were joined by the UAE, which has sought to support anti-Islamist rebel forces against the al-Assad regime and has participated in coalition air strikes against IS.[53] Lack of battlefield success by the FSA led the Saudis to shift some of their support to more-sectarian Salafi groups, such as the Islamic

---

[50] Smyth, 2015, p. 16. The Grand Ayatollah, the venerated Shi'a religious leader based in Najaf, Iraq, has refused to issue a fatwa urging Shi'a jihad in Syria. One might speculate that the Supreme Leader has left the issuance of projihad fatwas to subordinates to avoid open disagreement with the Grand Ayatollah.

[51] "Turkey Cracks Down on Foreign Fighters Crossing Border to Join ISIS," CBSnews.com, September 29, 2015.

[52] These militias were recently targeted in Russian air strikes. See Ihsaan Tharoor, "Syria's Turkmen Rebels, the Group at the Center of the Russia-Turkey Clash," *Washington Post*, November 24, 2015.

[53] Alissa Fromkin, "Part Three: UAE Foreign Policy in Iraq and Syria," *International Affairs Review*, Elliott School of International Affairs at George Washington University, March 5, 2015.

Front, but they continue to shun direct support of al-Qaeda–linked al-Nusra and certainly IS.[54] Conversely, Qatar, also a member of the anti-IS coalition, has supported Islamist rebels and reportedly is seeking to make al-Nusra more attractive as a "lesser evil" than IS.[55]

At the same time, however, both Saudi Arabia and Qatar have supported Jaish al-Islam and Arhar al-Sham, which have worked directly with al-Nusra and seek Shari'a law in all of Syria. The leader of Jaysh al-Islam in 2013 when it merged with the Syrian Islamic Front, Zahran Alloush—who became the Syrian Islamic Front's military commander and was killed on December 25, 2015, in what was believed to be a Russian air strike—had been considered a moderate opposition leader by the Saudis, as well as by Turkey and Qatar. But his rhetoric was salafist, virulently anti-Shi'a, and called for establishment of an Umayyad caliphate in the region. In a September 2013 video, Alloush stated, "We will bury the heads of impure Shi'a in Najaf, God willing. The Umayyad glory will return to the Levant in spite of you."[56] Alloush was reported to have met multiple times with al-Nusra leaders and provides an example of external support for sectarian Sunni actors in Syria.

Sunni clerics abroad have called for jihad against the Bashar al-Assad government and against Hezbollah, lacing their statements with anti-Shi'a and anti-Alawi rhetoric. One of the most renowned of these is Yusuf al-Qaradawi, the influential head of the International Union of Muslim Scholars, based in Qatar. Using the historical term for the Alawi sect in quoting Ibn Taymiyyah, he exclaimed in May 2013,

> The Nusayris are more disbelieving than the Jews and the Christians, as Shaykh al-Islam Ibn Taymiyyah said about them. We see them today killing people like mice and cats, by the thousands

---

[54]   Gause, 2014, pp. 6–7.

[55]   Yaroslav Trofimov, "To U.S. Allies, al-Qaeda Affiliate in Syria Becomes the Lesser Evil," *Wall Street Journal*, June 11, 2015.

[56]   Ali Mamouri, "Was Zahran Alloush Really a Moderate Leader?" *Al-Monitor*, January 14, 2016.

Sectarianism in Syria   93

and tens of thousands. Assad has come to rule by his own authority and with him his Nusayri sect.[57]

Qaradawi went on later that year to call on "every Sunni Muslim
with military training to go and fight Shi'a and Alawis in Syria," essentially calling for a jihad.[58] Such statements by influential Sunni clerics
have helped motivate foreign fighters to join the battle in Syria, often
with jihadist militias, including IS. According to one foreign fighter,
"The war in Syria is between the Alawi and Shi'a people and the Sunni.
We have to follow the orders of God to help [the Sunni]."[59] This atti-
tude is emblematic of the motivations of many foreign Sunni fighters
and has been contrasted with those of Syria-born Sunni rebels and
civilians who have particular political grievances against the Bashar al-
Assad government.[60] For Qaradawi and other Sunni clerics, "the Syrian
war is evidence of the Shi'a drive for power over the Sunnis, no matter
the cost."[61]

Regime and Opposition Elements Have Employed Sectarian-Related Assaults, but Much Violence Remains Indiscriminate

Violence and "cleansing" against Sunni and Alawi/Shi'a communities
have been committed in a number of cases by proregime militias on
one hand and rebel groups on the other, and these atrocities have been
accompanied by extreme anti-Shi'a and anti-Sunni rhetoric that fuels
a widening of the sectarian divide. It stokes fear that minority groups
(e.g., Alawis, Christians) are unable to safely live under Sunni rule, and
vice versa.

---

[57] Quoted in Farouk-Alli, 2014, p. 207.

[58] Quoted in David Schenker, "Qaradawi and the Struggle for Sunni Islam," *PolicyWatch*,
No. 2157, Washington Institute, October 16, 2013.

[59] Quoted in Vera Mironova and Sam Whitt, "A Glimpse into the Minds of Four Foreign
Fighters in Syria," *CTC Sentinel*, Vol. 7, No. 6, Combating Terrorism Center at West Point,
June 2014, p. 7.

[60] Mironova and Whitt, 2014, p. 7.

[61] Abdo, 2013, p. 42.

Bashar al-Assad's violent response to initially peaceful, nonsectarian demonstrations helped set the conditions for increasingly sectarian violence as the conflict extended over time and broadened in space. Hoping to quickly crush public dissent in these early stages, the al-Assad regime "would have to rely on predominantly Alawite military units, armed intelligence operatives, and criminal auxiliaries to put down an uprising that was mostly, although far from exclusively, Sunni Muslim."[62] In so doing, the regime exacerbated existing prejudices among the Sunni majority that rendered the entire Alawi community as complicit in regime survival and in maintaining Sunni inferiority politically and economically. It also helped both regime supporters and detractors to mobilize some constituencies based on sectarian identity.

Subsequent violence directed at homogeneous communities has helped fuel sectarian actions in the conflict. There are a number of examples of reported massacres that appear to be directed at opposing sects. The al-Assad regime and, in particular, its brutal *shabiha* paramilitary groups have instigated several widely reported and utilized instances of targeted attacks against Sunni civilians. In the small Sunni town of Taldou, near Houla northwest of Homs, 108 civilians—including 49 children and 34 women—were "summarily executed in two separate incidents" on May 25, 2012, by armed men who moved house to house late into the night.[63] It was alleged that these shooters were *shabiha* from nearby Alawi villages to the south of Houla. A second massacre occurred in nearby al-Qubeir, northwest of Hama, less than two weeks later. Seventy-eight civilians—most of the small village's inhabitants—were shot, beheaded, and burned. A UN mission to assess the site was initially blocked by the Syrian Army; when UN personnel finally were permitted to enter the town, no corpses were

---

[62] Frederic C. Hof, "Syria: Does the Threat of Sectarian 'Cleansing' Stay the West's Hand?" Atlantic Council, May 17, 2013.

[63] See Elizabeth A. Kennedy, "Syria Massacre Victims in Houla Executed, Says UN," *Huffington Post*, May 29, 2012; and "Houla: How a Massacre Unfolded," BBC News, June 8, 2012.

present. The massacre was again attributed to the *shabiha*.[64] A year later, in May 2013, some 150 civilians in the Sunni town of Bayda and the Sunni Ras al-Nabaa district of the city of Baniyas (both along the Mediterranean coast south of Latakia) were killed, this time reportedly by Syrian soldiers with *shabiha* involvement, also causing hundreds of Sunnis to flee their homes. Notably, this was followed by a joint call on YouTube from an Alawi militia leader and an Alawi religious figure for plans to "cleanse Baniyas of the traitors" and has been linked to Bashar al-Assad's alleged plan to secure an Alawi-dominated rump state in the coastal region in the event Damascus falls.[65]

Nonstate armed groups opposing the government—the vast majority of which are Sunni, whether secular or pious—have also engaged in sectarian-related violence. Generally, like their political and social expressions, self-proclaimed jihadists (e.g., al-Nusra, IS) tend to perpetrate the most egregious examples of this. Sunni extremists abducted at least 54 Alawi women and children during operations in the Latakia region in August 2013, and they were reportedly held by *mujahideen* in the Latakia countryside.[66] In February 2015, IS raided a number of rural Assyrian Christian villages west of Hasaka in northeastern Syria and kidnapped some 150 civilians, including children and the elderly.[67] Massacres against primarily Alawi and Christian communities have been reported, with 15 murdered in Homs in April 2012, 300 in Aqrab in December 2012, 16 in Maksar al-Hesan in September 2013, and 45 in Sadad in October 2013.[68] Also in 2013, a video posted by radical Sunni rebels of bodies of Shi'a massacred in Hatla was accompanied by

---

[64] See Rick Gladstone, "UN Monitors in Syria Find Grisly Traces of Massacre," *New York Times*, June 8, 2012; and Ruth Sherlock and Magdy Samaan, "Syria: Full Horror of al-Qubeir Massacre Emerges," *Telegraph*, June 7, 2012.

[65] Quoted in Elizabeth O'Bagy, "Syria Update: Assad Targets Sunni Along Syria's Coast," Institute for the Study of War, May 10, 2013.

[66] Human Rights Watch, *World Report 2015*, "Country Summary: Syria," January 2015, p. 5.

[67] According to the Syriac National Council of Syria. See Suleiman al-Khalidi, "Islamic State in Syria Abducts at Least 150 Christians," Reuters, February 25, 2015.

[68] Phillips, 2015, p. 360.

a militant calling them "dogs" and threatening the same fate to other Shi'a.[69]

However, while such examples of sectarian violence are prevalent in the rhetoric of groups seeking to mobilize adherents to their causes, they do not necessarily dominate the overall prosecution of security and combat operations in the Syrian Civil War. Killing of civilians has most often been indiscriminate. Human Rights Watch has noted,

> In 2014, Syria's armed conflict grew increasingly bloody with government and pro-government militias intensifying their attacks on civilian areas and continuing use of indiscriminate weapons. Government forces also continued to arbitrarily arrest, disappear, and torture detainees, many of whom died in detention. Non-state armed groups opposing the government also carried out serious abuses including deliberate and indiscriminate attacks on civilians, use of child soldiers, kidnapping, and torture in detention.[70]

Syrian government forces have used cluster munitions and barrel bombs in populated areas held by rebel groups and have enforced sieges that reportedly affect 200,000 civilians in an effort to starve them into submission. Nonstate armed groups have launched indiscriminate mortar and artillery attacks on civilian neighborhoods under government control that have "repeatedly hit known civilian objectives, including schools, mosques, and markets."[71] And, as noted earlier, intrasect fighting has occurred as well; for example, clashes between Alawi elites and government security forces occurred in Qardaha, hometown of the al-Assad family, in the fall of 2012 after prominent Alawi families took part in antiregime street protests.[72] More recently, in August 2014, the Syrian Observatory on Human Rights reported that IS executed

---

[69] Reese, 2013, p. 14.

[70] Human Rights Watch, 2015, p. 1.

[71] Human Rights Watch, 2015, p. 4.

[72] O'Bagy, 2013.

700 civilians from the Sunni al-Sheitaat tribe, which IS had been fighting in eastern Syria over two oil fields it had taken.[73]

There Are Key Constituencies Inside Syria Not Motivated by Sectarianism

The Alawis find themselves in the position of being inextricably linked to the fate of the regime, "which still strives to exploit sectarian solidarity to maintain its support base."[74] Yet there are Alawi groups that have expressed opposition to the regime and are calling for a unified, democratic Syria to follow the Bashar al-Assad regime. At the same time, there are Sunni-Arab communities that continue to support the al-Assad regime.

Toward the beginning of the conflict, an Alawi writer from Syria's coastal region exclaimed that it was not the jihadists persecuting her sect, but the security services and the state who were "making the Alawis line up behind the regime and defend it" despite the "state of tyranny, miserable circumstances and widespread corruption" the regime encouraged. She called on Syrians, particularly Alawis, to "smash the narrative of this criminal regime with the truth of the revolution. . . . This is a revolution and not a sectarian war."[75] Some Alawis, particularly among the rural poor and professional classes, have denounced the al-Assad government because of its clientelism and failure to provide adequate services.[76]

There remain important Sunni elements of Syrian society that support the minority-rule al-Assad regime and a number of Sunni-dominated groups opposing the regime that shun sectarian rhetoric and emphasize national unity, including Sunni tribes, the National

---

[73] Oliver Holmes and Suleiman al-Khalidi, "Islamic State Executed 700 People from Syrian Tribe: Monitoring Group," Reuters, August 16, 2014.

[74] Farouk-Alli, 2014, p. 221.

[75] From Samar Yazbek, *A Woman in the Crossfire: Diaries of the Syrian Revolution*, trans. Max Weiss, London: Haus Publishing, 2012, quoted in Jose Ciro Martinez, "Rebellion, Sectarian Slaughter or Civil War? Reading the Syrian Melee," *New Middle Eastern Studies*, Vol. 3, 2013, p. 5.

[76] Martinez, 2013, p. 10.

Coalition, and the FSA. The regime maintains loyalty from Sunni bureaucrats who rely on government paychecks and from some middle-class and wealthy Sunni merchants in Damascus and Aleppo. In largely Sunni Aleppo, when rebels attacked in 2012, Syria's largest city (and a financial center) was divided along economic lines, with the wealthy western sectors divided from the poorer east.[77] Tribal leadership in Syria has been a voice of unity across sectarian lines. The Syrian Arab Tribes Council, made up largely of Sunni tribes who oppose the Bashar al-Assad government, emphasizes national unity and avoids derogation of Shi'a or Alawis. In a June 2012 statement, they upheld

> the legitimate rights of the Syrian people with their right of self-defense and national resistance that aim[s] to bring down the usurped gang of the authority and all its symbols, along with the murderer of children Bashar al-Assad. . . . The council will continue to work in order to achieve this goal, and pay for all possible resources and precious sacrifice *for the homeland and its unity and cohesion of its components with all sects and religions and nationalities*[78] [emphasis added].

A prominent leader of the Syrian Arab Tribes Council and head of the Baqara tribe, Nawaf al-Bashir, criticized foreign backers of the al-Assad regime in nonsectarian terms as "nothing but mafia; they are tyrants, sinners, and murderers."[79] In 2014, the Sunni Baqara tribe battled IS, resulting in 400 deaths. This was followed by a truce, which IS threatened in January 2015 by abducting three of al-Bashir's sons.[80] The National Coalition and FSA maintain nonsectarian political agendas, but they have weakened in relation to militant Sunni Islamist groups.

---

[77] Phillips, 2015, p. 361.

[78] Syrian Arab Tribes Council, Facebook post, June 5, 2012.

[79] "I Praised Assad at Gunpoint, Says Syrian Tribal Leader," Reuters, January 17, 2012.

[80] See Redwan Bizar, "Islamic State Abducts Sons of Tribal Leader in Eastern Syria," ARA News, January 2, 2015a; and Redwan Bizar, "Islamic State Holds Meeting with Syrian Arab Tribes in Hasakah," ARA News, January 3, 2015b.

The Syrian Kurds tend toward the nonsectarian end of the spectrum in territories they administer. According to one Syrian Kurdish rebel leader,

> A year after we had liberated the Kurdish territories in Syria from the regime's troops, we realized that it would be necessary to set up an administration. . . . In doing so, we included all the territory's other ethnic groups, such as the Arabs, Assyrians, Turkmens.[81]

The Kurdish Democratic People's Union, with the help of its armed wing, the People's Protection Units (YPG), has consolidated control of a number of ethnically and religiously heterogeneous territories in northern Syria and provides basic services, including education in Arabic rather than Kurdish. In Kobane, where the Kurds make up about 97 percent of the indigenous population, there were some 300,000 internally displaced Syrians, mostly Arabs. According to one report, the displaced population lived in good conditions under Kurdish administration and continued to receive education in Arabic according to the Syrian curriculum—but without the subject of "nationalism."[82] Finally, Syrian Kurds have, in some cases, sought to promote cultural diversity. Large numbers of Syrian Kurdish school-age children reportedly called for cultural diversity and multilingualism on International Mother Language Day, stating that, "on this day we Kurds greet all nations in the world, but particularly our beloved Assyrian and Arab brothers and sisters here in Syria."[83] Yet it should be noted that the Kurds have mobilized along ethno-sectarian lines to counter IS and other extremist groups threatening Kurdish-dominated territories in northern and northeastern Syria and have drawn support

---

[81] "Austria: Syrian Kurds Fight al-Qa'idah on Europe's Behalf Too, Says Rebel Leader," *BBC Monitoring Europe—Political*, January 9, 2014.

[82] "Aleppo's Kurds: Living Under Siege," *Al-Akhbar* (English), January 12, 2014. This is akin to what the Iraqi Kurdistan Democratic Party did in Kurdish-controlled multiethnic regions of Iraq after the no-fly zone was implemented in 1991.

[83] "Minority Kurds Promote Cultural Diversity amid Syrian Civil War," video, *Your Middle East*, February 25, 2014.

from and coordinated with Iraqi Kurdish political parties and armed forces as well.

In sum, various internal and external actors in the Syrian conflict have found sectarianism to be a useful means of mobilization, and they have used it to sow fear among constituencies and demonize the "other." Early on, the regime of Bashar al-Assad used sectarian rhetoric to solidify the support of his Alawi base and to ensure that other minorities remained in his camp, or at least neutral. Sunni extremist groups like IS and al-Nusra—whose very ideologies glorify violence against other sects—have spread sectarianism against Alawis, Christians, Shi'a, and other minorities. External actors like Iran, Saudi Arabia, Turkey, and nonstate groups or individuals have, in various ways, promoted sectarian agendas as a means of defending or seeking to bring down the al-Assad regime. Both proregime and rebel groups have committed acts of sectarian-based violence and ethnic cleansing. Yet, in the midst of these heavily publicized acts of violence and rhetoric, there exist important groups in Syria that are not motivated by sectarianism and that do not fit neatly into constituencies ascribed to them by outside observers. Antiregime Alawis, proregime Sunnis, moderate rebel groups, and tribes whose allegiance is based on self-preservation all present counterpoints to what appears to be common wisdom about the Syrian conflict as a "sectarian war."

Conclusions and Implications of Sectarianism in the Syrian Conflict

While there has been a long history of sectarian identity in Syria, sectarianism has not been a primary feature of a heterogeneous Syrian society. But it has provided an underpinning that rises to greater prominence—and is given to exploitation—in times of strife. The al-Assads, while seeking to promote nationalism and secularism to obscure the fact of minority rule, have also exploited sectarian discourse to cement their hold on power. As strife intensified in 2011, sectarianism became an attractive tool for multiple competing political agendas.

Sectarianism plays an important role in fueling the Syrian conflict, but it has not been the only factor, nor is it uniformly the most important. On one hand, Hokayem notes, as the conflict goes on, Syrian society becomes ever more fragmented along communal lines:

> While the struggle is not primarily defined by sectarianism, the warring sides increasingly brandish communal identity as a tool of protection, mobilization, and exclusion. Distrust among and within Syria's various social and confessional groups has deepened. Many Sunnis perceive themselves to be the victims of a repression approved, explicitly or tacitly, by many members of the main minority groups and designed to keep them away from power. . . . On the other hand, minorities observe with alarm and trepidation the growing radicalism of the opposition and its assumed hostility towards them. Jihadi violence and isolated instances of sectarian revenge have had a major psychological impact on minorities. Many Alawi families have abandoned large cities for the safety of their villages and joined regime-backed militias, while many Christians have begun making plans for expatriation to Lebanon and beyond. Shi'a communities have built closer ties with Hezbollah in Lebanon and Iraqi Shi'a parties, while the Kurds have looked to the Iraqi example of de facto autonomy.[84]

The longer the conflict goes on, the more such tensions are likely to gain prominence as a motivating factor in the civil war and as an obstacle to a solution. Marc Lynch has termed this "ratcheting," whereby, "under conditions of state failure, uncertainty, violence, and fear . . . [i]t is far easier to generate sectarian animosities than it is to calm them down. . . . Identity entrepreneurs may think that they can turn the hatred on and off as it suits their interests, but at some point these identities become self-sustaining and internalized."[85]

---

[84] Hokayem, 2013, p. 192.

[85] Marc Lynch, "The Entrepreneurs of Cynical Sectarianism: Why the Middle East's Identity Conflicts Go Way Beyond the Sunni-Shiite Divide," *Foreign Policy*, No. 4, November 13, 2013, p. 5.

On the other hand, sectarianism did not create the revolt against Bashar al-Assad in 2011, and it is not the only factor fueling it. The conflict is too complex to explain away as a simple explosion of sectarianism with roots in distant history. Important constituencies support or oppose the regime across sectarian lines. External actors are exploiting communal identity to promote their own geostrategic agendas. And the considerable gains by the most-extreme elements of the opposition—namely, IS and al-Qaeda–linked groups—are as alarming to their coreligionists as they are to minority sects. Allegiances are crosscutting and are based also on political ideology, substate identity, geography, war experience, and economic motivation.[86] Given these other factors, it is not appropriate to term Syria's conflict a "sectarian war." Sectarianism is but one factor whose prominence varies depending on the actor, despite its high profile in reporting on the conflict.

An Extended Conflict Has the Potential to Raise Sectarian Motivation Inside and Outside Syria

Though the conclusion of this review of the Syrian Civil War suggests caution in attributing the conflict solely—or even primarily—to sectarian motivations, there is ample reason for concern that sectarianism could lead to worsening of the conflict or to outcomes that do not stop the violence and destabilize the rest of the region. At the time of this writing, the possibility of a negotiated settlement seems remote. Moreover, there does not appear to be a clearly dominant actor that can bring the conflict to a conclusion by force, and the parties that are more likely to control the state over time—the Syrian government and jihadist forces, with moderate opposition forces a distant third[87]—possess sectarian strategies or ideologies:

- A regime "win," in which government forces push rebel groups out of much of western, northern, and southern Syria, would leave

---

[86] Phillips, 2015, pp. 360–361.

[87] The U.S. effort to train and equip 3,000 moderate rebels by the end of 2015 (and 5,400 per year after that) appears to be faltering, with fewer than 100 volunteers undergoing training at the time of this writing. See Robert Burns, "U.S. Program to Train Syrian Rebels Has Fewer Than 100 Volunteers," *Stars and Stripes*, June 29, 2015.

minority rule in place in Damascus and would not address the political and economic grievances that fueled the revolt in the first place. Because of the "baggage" that years of conflict have created, sectarianism might play a more prominent part in government policy and rhetoric than it did prior to the revolt.

- A jihadist "win" in Syria would not end bloodshed or repression and would lead to more sectarian-based violence and policies. Violence and cleansing would likely be meted out against Alawis and Shi'a who had not fled, while any remaining Christians would be vulnerable to repression via the *jizya* tax and other administrative, economic, and social policies.

- Another possible outcome could include the emergence of ethno-sectarian territories, ministates, or fiefdoms due to battlefield results or regime collapse, with each entity situated in an area of relative homogeneity in ethnic, religious, or political terms—homogeneous historically or because of migration. Thus, an Alawi ministate could emerge in the coastal areas and Jabal Nusayriyyah, a Kurdish one in the northeast, a Sunni salafi-jihadist emirate in the north and east, and a Sunni statelet in the south between Damascus and the Golan Heights formed by less sectarian, Sunni-dominated opposition groups. Other minorities—Christians, Druze, Shi'a, and others—might reside in some combination of these areas or expatriate themselves. Violence would not necessarily cease, as each actor seeks to solidify or expand its own borders. The level of sectarianism within and among each of these fiefdoms would depend upon the actor.[88]

Notably, any of these outcomes would likely involve the additional mass transfer of populations, some of which would likely be sectarian-based.

The war has already provoked sectarian-related tension and strife outside Syria's borders. Jordan, Lebanon, and Turkey host hundreds of

---

[88] Drawn from a workshop on alternative Syrian futures held at RAND in December 2013. See Andrew M. Liepman, Brian Nichiporuk, and Jason Killmeyer, *Alternative Futures for Syria: Regional Implications and Challenges for the United States*, Santa Monica, Calif.: RAND Corporation, PE-129-RC, 2014, p. 3.

thousands of Syrian refugees. Many of these, especially in Jordan, are Sunni and have formed views of the war and of other Syrian sects based in no small part on the experiences that drove them from their homes. One scholar indicates that populations in Syria have experienced the war in different ways across the state and that "victims of ethno-sectarian violence are far more likely to view the conflict through a sectarian lens than those who have not been subjected to it."[89] Such views can affect populations' perceptions in host countries and complicate the development and implementation of policies; notably, 80 percent of refugees in Jordan live outside the refugee camps in towns and cities.[90] And in the event of repatriation, the possibility of reprisal killings and land disputes will be high.

The sectarian divide in the Persian Gulf—a divide that has roots in official policy in some states—is being exacerbated by the increasingly sectarian nature of the conflicts in both Syria and Iraq, as well as government worldviews that drive their approaches to those conflicts.[91] Saudi Arabia, Kuwait, and Bahrain have Sunni-dominated governments with significant Shi'a populations (and in the case of Bahrain, a Shi'a majority), and each faces spillover from the two conflicts. For example, IS claimed responsibility for a suicide bombing at a Shi'a mosque in Kuwait in late June 2015 that killed 27 people and wounded more than 200. Extremist fighters in Syria aim to continue the jihad and "free the Arabian Peninsula."[92] Sectarian tension could increase in those countries, leading to instability and violence like that seen recently in Yemen.

Lebanon, built upon a fragile sectarian balance, has already experienced increased instability and a growing inability to effectively govern its sovereign territory, particularly in the north. Fighting has broken out in the coastal city of Tripoli, as well as the Hezbollah redoubt in the Bekaa Valley, where the Shi'a group has allied with local Chris-

---

89 Phillips, 2015, p. 361.

90 Jasser, 2014, p. 65.

91 "Saudi Arabia Has a Shiite Problem," *Foreign Policy*, December 3, 2014.

92 Mironova and Whitt, 2014, p. 4.

tians and where Sunni leaders in nearby Arsal have openly supported the insurgency against Bashar al-Assad.[93] Shi'a political expressions in Lebanon describing the fight in Syria have taken on increasingly theological rather than geopolitical tones. In one Shi'a neighborhood in Beirut, for example, pamphlets explain the Syrian war in terms of the apocalypse—a fight against the *dajal* (the false messiah who will appear before the Day of Resurrection) that is linked with the return of the *mahdi* from Shi'a millenarianism and eschatology. Such imagery has attracted foreign Shi'a fighters to Syria from as far away as Pakistan and Azerbaijan.[94] Al-Nusra confirmed in March 2015 that it considers striking Hezbollah in Lebanon to be an objective because of Hezbollah's violence against Sunnis in Syria. Calling Hezbollah by the derogatory name Hezb Lat (Party of Lat, the pre-Islamic goddess of the Underworld), al-Nusra has stated that "this vexed Hezb Lat, that the Sunni people possess a thorn, so it incited the army to strike them. . . . It is no longer a secret to anyone what the Party [Hezbollah] commits against the Sunni people in Syria. Therefore, our objective in Lebanon at this stage is to hit the strongholds of the Iranian Hezbollah, for the party and whoever supports it is a legitimate target for us. . . . we collect our efforts to push away the assailing Nusayri enemy and its allies."[95] Lebanon, therefore, is highly vulnerable to the spread of sectarian violence from Syria.

Thus, while the Syrian conflict should not be considered a "sectarian war" whose foundation is based on confessional animosities, important parties to the conflict have used sectarianism effectively to mobilize constituencies. And there is ample reason to worry that sectarianism could grow internally the longer the conflict goes on—making it more intractable to a negotiated solution—and spread exter-

---

[93] Anne Barnard, "Sectarian Wedge Pushes from Syria to Lebanon," *New York Times*, October 27, 2014.

[94] "The Escalating Shia-Sunni Conflict: Assessing the Role of ISIS," Stimson Center Conference, Middle East Program, December 15, 2014.

[95] Al-Nusra, "Statement No. 24: Statement Clarifying What Came in the Interview of Sheikh Abu Malik al-Shami, May Allah Preserve Him," translated by SITE, March 15, 2015b.

nally to other parts of the region where important U.S. interests lie. Alternatives that involve a regime or jihadi "win," or a devolution of Syria into statelets with continued violence, are not agreeable outcomes in this context. Therefore, the sooner the conflict can be brought to an acceptable conclusion, the better.

This suggests two policy paths for the United States. The first involves substantial support to moderate anti–al-Assad groups in Syria—not only so-called moderate rebels, but also other groups with nonsectarian grievances, including Alawis and tribes—in combination with redoubled efforts to bring about a negotiated solution. U.S. support should be perceived as equitable and nonsectarian. The second requires development of an effective strategy for the defeat of IS and others in Syria with whom it is not possible to negotiate because of their extremist agendas and exclusively sectarian ideologies. Failure to pursue these two tracks may lead to increased sectarianism in a conflict that could last many years longer. That said, managing the balance between seeking the fall of Bashar al-Assad and the denuding of IS will continue to be a severe challenge.

CHAPTER FIVE

Conclusion and Policy Implications

Sectarianism is often claimed to be the root cause of current conflicts in the Middle East. Although sectarianism does play a major role, we argue against the depiction of it as one ancient, continuous, and intractable conflict between the Sunni and Shi'a over theological disputes.

Taking a historical approach and using diverse primary and secondary sources, this report demonstrates that sectarianism is a complex political phenomenon shaped more by social, economic, political, and other practical considerations than by theological disagreements or religious animosity. As detailed in the history of Sunni-Shi'a conflict in the region, the examination of Syria and Iraq as case studies, and the discussion of regional sectarian competition, specific nonreligious factors drive and exacerbate sectarianism and sectarian conflict rather than sectarianism driving these conflicts.

State governments; regional sectarian actors, such as Saudi Arabia and Iran; and transnational extremist groups, such as IS, utilize sectarian rhetoric or action for their own political purposes. State repression often causes individuals or groups within civil society to respond to a perceived or real threat to their sectarian identities. For example, the 2011 Syrian Civil War began as a series of political demonstrations against the Alawi-led state but morphed into a conflict with sectarian overtones as the Bashar al-Assad regime shot demonstrators en masse and released Islamist prisoners, precipitating the Syrian war we witness today. Additionally, while not the cause of sectarianism, regional sectarian actors and transnational extremist groups exacerbate preexisting sectarian divisions and cause conflicts to worsen. One sees this in both Iraq and Syria.

It seems undeniable that ethno-sectarianism will play a strong and perhaps dominant role in Iraqi politics, at least for the foreseeable future. Nearly two centuries of Sunni oppression of the Shi'a will not soon be forgotten, nor will the intense violence of the 2006–2007 civil war or the more-recent government oppression of Sunnis. However, the history of sectarianism in Iraq suggests that it is not too late to avert state fragmentation. Sunni identity in Iraq is not entirely about Sunni Islam, and the Sunnis did not identify primarily along sectarian lines until well into the past decade. This was perhaps also true of Shi'a Iraqis in the early 1800s: There was a point at which the Ottoman government could have been more inclusive of the Shi'a rather than forcing them to self-organize along sectarian lines. In 2015, Prime Minister al-Abadi has publicly acknowledged that government reform is the key to stability and state survival and that reconciling with the Sunnis is central to this effort.

While poor governance and disastrous intervention intensified sectarianism in Iraq, improved governance and less meddlesome external support might offer a recipe for eventual stability. This may be true in Iraq and in other areas in the Middle East currently riven by sectarian conflict.

Despite efforts in Syria by several internal and external parties to the civil war to exploit sectarian tension to promote their own political agendas and mobilize constituencies, it would be simplistic to refer to sectarianism as the main source of the uprising against Bashar al-Assad or as the sole motivator of continuing violence. The anti–al-Assad uprising began as a cross-sectarian rebellion, and, even now, there are key constituencies inside Syria (progovernment Sunnis, antigovernment Alawis, and groups with nonsectarian agendas) not motivated by sectarianism. Allegiances are crosscutting and are based also on political ideology, substate identity, geography, war experience, and economic drivers.

However, though we suggest caution in attributing the conflict solely—or even primarily—to sectarian motivations, there is ample reason for concern that sectarianism could make the war more intractable to a negotiated solution and lead to worsening of the conflict or to outcomes that do not stop the violence and destabilize other parts of the region where there are vital U.S. interests. Alternatives that involve a regime or jihadi "win" or a devolution of Syria into statelets with continued violence will not stanch growing sectarianism in this context. Therefore, the sooner the conflict can be brought to a conclusion that addresses mainstream Syrian grievances and interests, the better.

Having examined how sectarianism can manifest differently in different places, the U.S. government, especially the U.S. Army, should consider several factors when determining the best policy for involvement in conflicts in which sectarianism is part of the equation. Sectarianism needs to be viewed as a complex political problem and, thus, needs comprehensive policy prescriptions.

Acknowledge Limits on the U.S. Ability to Influence the Role of Sectarianism in Middle East Conflicts

First and foremost, it is important for U.S. policymakers to internalize the fact that the power of the United States to actively and directly dissipate sectarianism as a factor in regional conflict is limited. U.S. policies and actions can seek to support non- or pansectarian agendas and avoid the appearance of favoritism, but they are not likely to play a direct role in either broadening or contracting sectarian identity as a motivator of violence. It is difficult to foresee anything but a cessation of hostilities and a broad-based solution to the conflicts (as well as containment or elimination of the most-extremist groups, such as IS) that would be an effective counter to growing sectarianism. Recent U.S. efforts to forge a common approach to UN-sponsored peace talks on Syria and support for Iraqi operations against IS are important in this regard. Our policy prescriptions therefore focus on ensuring that U.S. policies do not exacerbate sectarianism or play into sectarian narratives that already exist on all sides of the conflicts. Where possible, we recommend that the United States use its influence to persuade friends in the region to consider less sectarian narratives of the conflicts in pursuit of equitable solutions.

The U.S. presence in the region and the U.S. Army's role in leading the coalition against IS do provide the United States influence and leverage, and U.S. policymakers should exploit its position to the extent practicable to shape a shared strategic vision among its friends and allies that crosses sectarian boundaries.

Avoid Oversimplification

Sectarianism is not the same in each country or region, and it manifests itself differently in different places. Policymakers need to be aware of this to avoid making generalizations about the role of sectarianism in Middle East conflicts in order to tailor a unique and effective approach to each conflict.

U.S. decisionmakers should avoid placing people and groups into large, simplified categories for easier identification. Instead, they should identify individuals and groups with which the United States can find common ground on political objectives. This will take long-term, wide-scale intelligence collection and in-depth analysis.

Address Political Issues at Hand, Given That Sectarianism Is Usually a Symptom of Conflict, Not a Cause of It

It is important to note that, while the political environment of the region currently lends itself to a surge in sectarianism, sectarianism might not be the most important way in which to understand regional conflict, which, in its most simplified form, looks like solely sectarian conflict. Viewing regional conflict through a strictly sectarian lens could be a major pitfall for policymakers, especially because sects are not homogeneous blocs.

U.S. decisionmakers should identify nonsectarian motivations to work with those "acting outside of their sect." This entails cooperating as much as possible with current government and local actors to assuage practical concerns contributing to conflict.

The United States Should Not Choose Sides or Be Perceived to Be Choosing Sides

Sectarianism can be best described as a two-pronged phenomenon: internal and external sectarianism. Internal sectarianism is sectarian conflict or rhetoric on an intrastate level, usually from a country's state leaders, religious leaders, or oppositionists who are using sectarian identity for their own political purposes. For policymakers, internal sectarianism causes a dilemma of whom to support and whether to get involved at all; as history has too often shown, foreign favoritism toward one side of an internal political conflict can backfire, especially if that conflict is based on sectarian divisions. Any involvement must be carefully considered, given that choosing can make the situation worse and possibly undermine both U.S. national security interests and the interests of the groups in conflict.

Explicitly Utilize Train-and-Equip and Coalition Efforts to Promote Nonsectarian Narratives and Cross-Sectarian Dialogue

The U.S. Army is at the forefront of efforts to advise, train, and equip forces fighting IS in Syria and Iraq, and its presence as part of the coalition provides an opportunity to forge cross-sectarian partnerships and to promote dialogue among Shi'a, Sunni, and other sects in the region.

The Army could begin to view training and equipping programs not just as a means to increase military capability but also as a way of shaping partners' perception of the threat and of the utility of working across sectarian lines. Inculcation of professionalism and respect for human rights are among the key counters to the sectarianism that appears to be increasing in the region. Army advisers can also serve as interlocutors between anti-IS fighters who are from different sects or between local groups and the Iraqi government.

Do Not Contribute to the Institutionalization of Sectarianism in State and Local Institutions

U.S. decisionmakers should avoid policies that institutionalize sectarianism in local or state institutions. This entails working with leaders committed to pursuing nonsectarian and pluralistic policies. The United States should support and encourage local and state institutions and provide incentives across the sects to achieve participation and inclusiveness in governing institutions.

Institutions throughout the region have been undergoing transition since the Arab Uprisings in 2011. The United States must take the long view that this period of transition is likely to be unstable and often violent. But policies should also be developed with a view to shaping longer-term outcomes. In Iraq, this means encouraging programs that seek to undo the damage of years of Iraqi government alienation of the Sunni minority and reintegrating Sunnis into Iraqi society and government and, most importantly, the Iraqi Army.

Determine Unique Approaches to Mitigate the Sectarianizing Policies of External Sectarian Actors

External sectarianism takes place on an interstate level and involves a sectarian actor's encouragement of sectarian divisions in foreign countries internally for its own political purposes. The continued regionalization of sectarianism has the potential to cause conflict in individual states to spread to other states by way of sectarian groups being incited internally by foreign sectarian conflicts or by way of external sectarian encouragement. It is important to note that many U.S. partners in the region—especially the Gulf Arab states—see the conflicts and even their foreign policies through a largely sectarian lens. U.S. policymakers should encourage alternative narratives in interactions with these partners, including through senior leader engagements on political and military matters.

Bibliography

Al-Abadi, Haider, "PM's 1st Package of Reforms to COM," official text, Government of Iraq, August 9, 2015. As of August 15, 2015: http://pmo.iq/pme/press2015en/9-8-20152en.htm

Abbas, Mushreq, "Iraq's 'Sunni' Rebellion Shows Splits Between ISIS, Others," *Al-Monitor*, June 24, 2014.

Abdo, Geneive, *The New Sectarianism: The Arab Uprisings and the Rebirth of the Shi'a Sunni Divide*, Washington, D.C.: Brookings Institution, 2013.

Abdul-Ahad, Geith, "Syria's al-Nusra Front—Ruthless, Organised and Taking Control," *Guardian*, July 10, 2013. As of June 17, 2015: http://www.theguardian.com/world/2013/jul/10/syria-al-nusra-front-jihadi

Abdul-Jabar, Faleh, and Hosham Dawod, *Tribes and Power: Nationalism and Ethnicity in the Middle East*, London: Saqi Books, 2003.

Abdulla, Namo, "The View from Kurdistan: Divide Iraq in Order to Save It," *Al Jazeera*, June 13, 2014. As of June 7, 2015: http://www.aljazeera.com/indepth/opinion/2014/06/iraq-isil-kurds-201461274633487455.html

Adams, Doris G., "Current Population Trends in Iraq," *Middle East Journal*, Vol. 10, No. 2, 1956, pp. 151–165.

Alaaldin, Ramj, "If Iraq Is to Survive, Then It Must Be Divided into Separate Regions," *Independent*, August 17, 2014. As of June 7, 2015: http://www.independent.co.uk/voices/comment/if-iraq-is-to-survive-then-it-must-be-split-into-ethnic-and-religious-regions-9674794.html

Ala Hamoudi, Haider, *Negotiating in Civil Conflict: Constitutional Construction and Imperfect Bargaining in Iraq*, Chicago: University of Chicago Press, 2014, Kindle.

Arango, Tim, "Dozens Killed in Battles Across Iraq as Sunnis Escalate Protests Against Government," *New York Times*, April 23, 2013. As of July 8, 2015: http://www.nytimes.com/2013/04/24/world/middleeast/clashes-at-sunni-protest-site-in-iraq.html

Armstrong, Karen, *Islam: A Short History*, New York: Modern Library, 2002.

"Assad: Takfiri Terrorism Targets Diverse Social, Cultural Fabric of Region," Syrian Arab News Agency, June 11, 2015.

"Austria: Syrian Kurds Fight al-Qa'idah on Europe's Behalf Too, Says Rebel Leader," BBC Monitoring Europe—Political, January 9, 2014.

Baram, Amatzia, "Neotribalism in Iraq: Saddam Hussein's Tribal Policies 1991–1996," *International Journal of Middle East Studies*, No. 29, 1997, pp. 1–31.

Barnard, Anne, "Sectarian Wedge Pushes from Syria to Lebanon," *New York Times*, October 27, 2014.

Barwari, Delovan, "Partition Will Help End the Turmoil in Iraq," *Jerusalem Post*, March 8, 2015. As of June 7, 2015:
http://www.jpost.com/Opinion/Partition-will-help-end-the-turmoil-in-Iraq-393315

Barzegar, Kayhan, "Iran's Foreign Policy in Post-Invasion Iraq," *Middle East Policy*, Vol. 15, No. 4, 2008, pp. 47–58.

Batutu, Hanna, *The Old Social Classes and the Revolutionary Movement of Iraq*, Princeton, N.J.: Princeton University Press, 1978, Kindle.

———, *Syria's Peasantry, the Descendants of Its Lesser Rural Notables, and Their Politics*, Princeton, N.J.: Princeton University Press, 1999.

Bhalla, Reva, "Making Sense of the Syrian Crisis," *Stratfor*, May 5, 2011

Bizar, Redwan, "Islamic State Abducts Sons of Tribal Leader in Eastern Syria," ARA News, January 2, 2015a.

———, "Islamic State Holds Meeting with Syrian Arab Tribes in Hasakah," ARA News, January 3, 2015b.

Boghani, Priyanka, "In Their Own Words: Sunnis on Their Treatment in Maliki's Iraq," Public Broadcasting Service, October 28, 2014. As of July 8, 2015:
http://www.pbs.org/wgbh/pages/frontline/iraq-war-on-terror/rise-of-isis/in-their-own-words-sunnis-on-their-treatment-in-malikis-iraq/

Bradley, Matt, and Ghassan Adnan, "Shiite Militias Win Bloody Battles in Iraq, Show No Mercy," *Wall Street Journal*, December 5, 2014:
http://www.wsj.com/articles/shiite-militias-win-bloody-battles-in-iraq-show-no-mercy-1417804464

Brancati, Dawn, "Can Federalism Stabilize Iraq?" *Washington Quarterly*, Vol. 27, No. 2, 2004, pp. 5–21.

Burns, Robert, "U.S. Program to Train Syrian Rebels Has Fewer Than 100 Volunteers," *Stars and Stripes*, June 29, 2015.

Caris, Charles C., and Samuel Reynolds, *ISIS Governance in Syria*, Middle East Security Report 22, Institute for the Study of War, July 2014.

Çetinsaya, Gökhan, "The Caliph and Mujtahids: Ottoman Policy Towards the Shiite Community of Iraq in the Late Nineteenth Century," *Middle Eastern Studies*, Vol. 41, No. 4, 2005, pp. 561–574.

Chivers, C. J., "Answering a Cleric's Call, Iraqi Shiites Take Up Arms," *New York Times*, June 21, 2014. As of August 16, 2015: http://www.nytimes.com/2014/06/22/world/middleeast/iraq-militia.html

Choksy, Jamsheed K., and Carol E. B. Choksy, "Defeat ISIS, but Let Iraq Split," *World Affairs*, undated. As of June 7, 2015: http://www.worldaffairsjournal.org/article/defeat-isis-let-iraq-split

CIA—*See* U.S. Central Intelligence Agency.

Coalition Provisional Authority, "Coalition Provisional Authority Order Number 1: De-Ba'athification of Iraqi Society," Baghdad, Iraq, 2003.

Cockburn, Patrick, *Muqtada: Muqtada al-Sadr, the Shia Revival, and the Struggle for Iraq*, New York: Scribner, 2008.

Cole, Juan, *Marsh Arab Rebellion: Grievance, Mafias and Militias in Iraq*, Fourth Wadie Jwaideh Memorial Lecture, Department of Near Eastern Languages and Cultures, Indiana University, Bloomington, Ind., 2008.

Cole, Juan R. I., and Moojan Momen, "Mafia, Mob, and Shiism in Iraq: The Rebellion of Ottoman Karbala, 1824–1843," *Past and Present*, No. 112, 1986, pp. 112–143.

Coles, Isabel, "Iraq Chaos Fuels Kurds' Independence Dream, but Hurdles Remain," Reuters, July 6, 2014. As of August 16, 2015: http://www.reuters.com/article/2014/07/06/ us-iraq-security-kurds-idUSKBN0FB0Y620140706

Connable, Ben, *Military Intelligence Fusion for Complex Operations*, Santa Monica, Calif.: RAND Corporation, OP-377-RC, 2012. As of August 1, 2018: https://www.rand.org/pubs/occasional_papers/OP377.html

———, "A Long Term Strategy for a Democratic Iraq," *War on the Rocks*, June 30, 2014. As of August 6, 2015: http://warontherocks.com/2014/06/a-long-term-strategy-for-a-democratic-iraq/

Cooper, Andrew Scott, "Showdown at Doha: The Secret Oil Deal That Helped Sink the Shah of Iran," *Middle East Journal*, Vol. 62, No. 4, August 2008, pp. 567–591.

CPA—*See* Coalition Provisional Authority.

Dale, Stephen F., *The Muslim Empires of the Ottomans, Safavids, and Mughals*, New York: Cambridge University Press, 2010. As of August 16, 2015: https://books.google.com/books?isbn=0813313597

Dawisha, Adeed, "'Identity' and Political Survival in Saddam's Iraq," *Middle East Journal*, Vol. 53, No. 4, 1999, pp. 553–567.

————, *Arab Nationalism in the Twentieth Century: From Triumph to Despair*, Princeton, N.J.: Princeton University Press, 2003, Kindle.

————, *Iraq: A Political History*, Princeton, N.J.: Princeton University Press, 2009, Kindle.

Dawood, Hosham, "The 'State-ization' of the Tribe and the Tribalization of the State: The Case of Iraq," in Faleh Abdul-Jabar and Hosham Dawood, *Tribes and Power: Nationalism and Ethnicity in the Middle East*, London: Saqi Books, 2003, pp. 83–108.

Devlin, John F., "The Baath Party: Rise and Metamorphosis," *American Historical Review*, Vol. 96, No. 5, 1991, pp. 1396–1407.

Dodge, Toby, *Inventing Iraq: The Failure of Nation Building and a History Denied*, New York: Columbia University Press, 2003.

————, *Iraq: From War to a New Authoritarianism*, London: International Institute for Strategic Studies, 2012.

————, "Seeking to Explain the Rise of Sectarianism in the Middle East: The Case Study of Iraq," Project on Middle East Political Science, March 19, 2014.

Edelman, Marc, "Social Movements Changing Paradigms and Forms of Politics," *Annual Review of Anthropology*, Vol. 30, 2000, pp. 285–317.

Eich, Thomas, "Patterns of the 1920 Rising in Iraq, the Rifaiyya Tariqa and Shiism," *Arabica*, Vol. 56, No. 1, 2009, pp. 112–119.

Eppel, Michael, *Iraq from Monarchy to Tyranny: From the Hashemites to the Rise of Saddam*, Gainesville, Fla.: University Press of Florida, 2004.

Farouk-Alli, Aslam, "Sectarianism in Alawi Syria: Exploring the Paradoxes of Politics and Religion," *Journal of Muslim Minority Affairs*, Vol. 34, No. 3, 2014, pp. 207–226.

Farouk-Sluglett, Marion, and Peter Sluglett, "The Historiography of Modern Iraq," *American Historical Review*, Vol. 96, No. 4, 1991, pp. 1408–1421.

Felter, Joseph, and Brian Fishman, *Iranian Strategy in Iraq: Politics and "Other Means,"* West Point, N.Y.: Combating Terrorism Center, U.S. Military Academy, October 13, 2008.

Fildis, Ayse Tekdal, "Roots of Alawite-Sunni Rivalry in Syria," *Middle East Policy Council*, Vol. 19, No. 2, Summer 2012

Fischer, Hannah, *Iraqi Civilian Death Estimates*, Washington, D.C.: Congressional Research Service, RS22537, August 27, 2008.

"Foreign Fighters Flow to Syria," *Washington Post*, October 11, 2014.

Fromkin, Alissa, "Part Three: UAE Foreign Policy in Iraq and Syria," *International Affairs Review*, Elliott School of International Affairs at George Washington University, March 5, 2015.

Fuller, Graham E., "Why Does ISIS Hate Shi'a?" lobelog.com, December 17, 2014.

Gause, Gregory F., *Beyond Sectarianism: The New Middle East Cold War*, Washington, D.C.: Brookings Institution, 2014.

Gengler, Justin L., "Understanding Sectarianism in the Persian Gulf," in *Sectarian Politics in the Persian Gulf*, Lawrence G. Potter, ed., London: Hurst and Company, 2013, pp. 31–66.

Gladstone, Rick, "UN Monitors in Syria Find Grisly Traces of Massacre," *New York Times*, June 8, 2012

Goldberg, Jeffrey, "After Iraq," *Atlantic*, January–February 2008. As of June 20, 2015:
http://www.theatlantic.com/magazine/archive/2008/01/after-iraq/306577/

———, "The New Map of the Middle East," *Atlantic*, June 19, 2014. As of June 20, 2015:
http://www.theatlantic.com/international/archive/2014/06/
the-new-map-of-the-middle-east/373080/

Government of Iraq, "Agrarian Reform Law of the Republic of Iraq," No. 30, Baghdad, Iraq, October 1958.

Gritten, David, "Long Path to Iraq's Sectarian Split," BBC News, February 25, 2006. As of June 20, 2015:
http://news.bbc.co.uk/2/hi/middle_east/4750320.stm

Haddad, Fanar, *Sectarianism in Iraq: Antagonistic Visions of Unity*, Oxford, UK: Oxford University Press, 2011, Kindle.

———, "Sectarian Relations and Sunni Identity in Post–Civil War Iraq," in Lawrence G. Potter, ed., *Sectarian Politics in the Persian Gulf*, London: Hurst and Company, 2013, pp. 67–115.

———, "Reinventing Sunni Identity in Iraq After 2003," *Current Trends in Islamist Ideology*, Vol. 17, 2014, pp. 70–101.

Haddad, Fanar, and Sajjad Rizvi, "Fitting Baghdad In," in Reidar Visser and Gareth Stansfield, eds., *An Iraq of Its Regions: Cornerstones of a Federal Democracy?* New York: Columbia University Press, 2008, pp. 51–74.

Harari, Michal, "Status Update: Shi'a Militias in Iraq," Institute for the Study of War, backgrounder, 2010. As of June 4, 2015:
http://www.understandingwar.org/sites/default/files/
Backgrounder_ShiaMilitias.pdf

Harding, Luke, Miriam Elder, and Peter Beaumont, "Assad Losing Syria War, Russia Admits for First Time," *Guardian*, December 13, 2012.

Heydemann, Steven, *Authoritarianism in Syria: Institutions and Social Conflict 1946–1970*, Cornell University Press: Ithaca, New York, 1999.

———, "Syria's Uprising: Sectarianism, Regionalisation, and State Order in the Levant," Fundación para las Relaciones Internacionales y el Diálogo Exterior working paper 119, May 2013.

"Hezbollah, Syrian Army Advance in Jarajir Barrens," *al-Manar*, June 12, 2015.

Hof, Frederic C., "Syria: Does the Threat of Sectarian 'Cleansing' Stay the West's Hand?" Atlantic Council, May 17, 2013.

Hokayem, Emile, *Syria's Uprising and the Fracturing of the Levant, Adelphi Series*, Vol. 53, No. 438, June 14, 2013, p. 18.

Holmes, Oliver, and Suleiman al-Khalidi, "Islamic State Executed 700 People from Syrian Tribe: Monitoring Group," Reuters, August 16, 2014.

Hornsey, Matthew J., "Social Identity Theory and Self-Categorization Theory: A Historical Overview," *Social and Personality Psychology Compass*, Vol. 2, No. 1, 2008, pp. 204–222.

"Houla: How a Massacre Unfolded," BBC News, June 8, 2012.

Hudson, Michael C., "Democracy and Social Mobilization in Lebanese Politics," *Comparative Politics*, Vol. 1, No. 2, 1969, pp. 245–263.

Human Rights Watch, *World Report 2015*, "Country Summary: Syria," January 2015, p. 5.

Hunt, Emily, "Zarqawi's 'Total War' on Iraqi Shiites Exposes a Divide Among Sunni Jihadists," Washington, D.C.: Washington Institute, November 15, 2005. As of August 16, 2015:
http://www.washingtoninstitute.org/policy-analysis/view/
zarqawis-total-war-on-iraqi-shiites-exposes-a-divide-among-sunni-jihadists

Husayn, Ayad Mahmud, "Are the Shia Really the Majority in Iraq?" in Arabic, *Al-Arab News*, April 11, 2005. As of June 24, 2015:
http://alarabnews.com/alshaab/2005/04-11-2005/19.htm

"I Praised Assad at Gunpoint, Says Syrian Tribal Leader," Reuters, January 17, 2012.

Izady, Michael, "Syria: Religious Composition (Summary)," map, Columbia University Gulf 2000 Project, 2015. As of August 16, 2015:
http://gulf2000.columbia.edu/images/maps/Syria_Religion_summary_lg.png

Jabar, Faleh A., "Sheikhs and Ideologues: Deconstruction and Reconstruction of Tribes Under Patrimonial Totalitarianism in Iraq, 1968–1998," in Faleh Abdul-Jabar and Hosham Dawood, *Tribes and Power: Nationalism and Ethnicity in the Middle East*, London: Saqi Books, 2003, pp. 53–81.

Jansen, Michael, "Repression by Iraq's Shia Regime Sparks Sunni Revolt," *Irish Times*, January 4, 2014. As of July 1, 2015:
http://www.irishtimes.com/news/world/middle-east/
repression-by-iraq-s-shia-regime-sparks-sunni-revolt-1.1643809

Jensen, Sterling, *Iraqi Narratives of the Anbar Awakening*, London: King's College, thesis, 2014.

Kalyvas, Stathis N., and Matthew Adam Kocher, "Ethnic Cleavages and Irregular War: Iraq and Vietnam," *Politics and Society*, Vol. 35, No. 2, 2007, pp. 183–233.

Karsh, Efraim, "Geopolitical Determinism: The Origins of the Iran-Iraq War," *Middle East Journal*, Vol. 44, No. 2, 1990, pp. 256–268.

Kennedy, Elizabeth A., "Syria Massacre Victims in Houla Executed, Says UN," *Huffington Post*, May 29, 2012

Khadim, Abbas, *Reclaiming Iraq: The 1920 Revolution and the Founding of the Modern State*, Austin, Texas: University of Texas Press, 2012.

al-Khalidi, Suleiman, "Islamic State in Syria Abducts at Least 150 Christians," Reuters, February 25, 2015.

Khalilzad, Zalmay, "Get Ready for Kurdish Independence," *New York Times*, July 13, 2014. As of August 16, 2015:
http://www.nytimes.com/2014/07/14/opinion/iraqs-urgent-need-for-unity.html

Knights, Michael, "The JRTN Movement and Iraq's Next Insurgency," West Point, N.Y.: Combating Terrorism Center, 2011.

Knights, Michael, Philip Smyth, and Ahmad Ali, "Iranian Influence in Iraq: Between Balancing and Hezbollahzation?" Washington, D.C.: Washington Institute, June 21, 2015. As of August 15, 2015:
http://www.washingtoninstitute.org/policy-analysis/view/
iraq-and-iranian-influence-between-balancing-and-hezbollah-ization

Kumaraswamy, P. R., "Who Am I? The Identity Crisis in the Middle East," *Middle East Review of International Affairs*, Vol. 10, No. 1, 2006, pp. 63–73.

Lawrence, Quil, "U.S. Sees New Threat in Iraq from Sufi Sect," National Public Radio, June 17, 2009. As of August 6, 2015:
http://www.npr.org/templates/story/story.php?storyId=105507397

"Lazma Law No. 51 of 1932," *Iraq Government Gazette*, No. 23, June 5, 1932, pp. 423–424.

Landis, Joshua, "The Syrian Uprising of 2011: Why the Asad Regime Is Likely to Survive to 2013," *Middle East Policy Council*, Vol. XIX, No. 1, Spring 2012, p. 6.

League of Nations, "Mandate for Syria and the Lebanon," London, July 24, 1922.

Legrand, Felix, "The Colonial Strategy of ISIS in Syria," *Arab Reform Initiative: Policy Alternatives*, June 2014, p. 6.

Leland, John, and Khalid D. Ali, "Anbar Province, Once a Hotbed of Iraqi Insurgency, Demands a Say on Resources," *New York Times*, October 27, 2010. As of August 16, 2015:
http://www.nytimes.com/2010/10/27/world/middleeast/27anbar.html

Liepman, Andrew M., Brian Nichiporuk, and Jason Killmeyer, *Alternative Futures for Syria: Regional Implications and Challenges for the United States*, Santa Monica, Calif.: RAND Corporation, PE-129-RC, 2014. As of August 3, 2018: https://www.rand.org/pubs/perspectives/PE129.html

Lipka, Michael, "The Sunni-Shia Divide: Where They Live, What They Believe and How They View Each Other," Pew Research Center, June 18, 2014.

Lister, Tim, "Iraq to Split in Three: So Why Not?" CNN, July 8, 2014. As of June 7, 2015: http://www.cnn.com/2014/07/07/world/meast/iraq-division-lister/

Lukitz, Liora, *Iraq: The Search for National Identity*, Portland, Ore.: Frank Cass and Co., 1995.

Lynch, Marc, "The Entrepreneurs of Cynical Sectarianism: Why the Middle East's Identity Conflicts Go Way Beyond the Sunni-Shiite Divide," *Foreign Policy*, No. 4, November 13, 2013, p. 5.

Al-Mahmud, Abdulaziz, "New Evidence . . . for the Sunni Majority in Iraq," in Arabic, Defense Network for the Sunnis, March 9, 2010. As of June 29, 2015: http://www.dd-sunnah.net/records/view/action/view/id/2659/

Makiya, Kanan, *Republic of Fear: The Politics of Modern Iraq*, Berkeley, Calif.: University of California Press, 1989 (1998 edition).

Mamouri, Ali, "Was Zahran Alloush Really a Moderate Leader?" *Al-Monitor*, January 14, 2016.

Marr, Phebe, *The Modern History of Iraq*, Boulder, Colo.: Westview Press, 2012.

Martin, Richard C., "Empires: Ottoman," in Richard C. Martin, ed., *Encyclopedia of Islam and the Muslim World*, Vol. 1, New York: Macmillan Reference USA, 2004, pp. 214–217.

Martinez, Jose Ciro, "Rebellion, Sectarian Slaughter or Civil War? Reading the Syrian Melee," *New Middle Eastern Studies*, Vol. 3, 2013.

Marschall, Christin, *Iran's Persian Gulf Policy: From Khomeini to Khatami*, New York: Routledge, 2003

McCarthy, John D., and Mayer N. Zald, "Resource Mobilization and Social Movements: A Partial Theory," *American Journal of Sociology*, Vol. 82, No. 6, 1977, pp. 1212–1241.

Milani, Mohsen, "Why Tehran Won't Abandon Assad(ism)," *Washington Quarterly*, Vol. 36, No. 4, Spring 2013, pp. 79–93.

"Minority Kurds Promote Cultural Diversity amid Syrian Civil War," video, *Your Middle East*, February 25, 2014.

Mironova, Vera, and Sam Whitt, "A Glimpse into the Minds of Four Foreign Fighters in Syria," *CTC Sentinel*, Vol. 7, No. 6, Combating Terrorism Center at West Point, June 2014, p. 7. As of October 22, 2015:
https://www.ctc.usma.edu/
posts/a-glimpse-into-the-minds-of-four-foreign-fighters-in-syria

Moniquet, Claude, "The Involvement of Salafism/Wahhabism in the Support and Supply of Arms to Rebel Groups Around the World," European Parliament Policy Department, June 11, 2013.

Montgomery, Gary W., and Timothy S. McWilliams, eds., *Al-Anbar Awakening Volume II: Iraqi Perspectives from Insurgency to Counterinsurgency in Iraq, 2004–2009*, Quantico, Va.: Marine Corps University Press, 2009.

Nader, Alireza, Ali G. Scotten, Ahmad Rahmani, Robert Stewart, and Leila Mahnad, *Iran's Influence in Afghanistan: Implications for the U.S. Drawdown*, Santa Monica, Calif.: RAND Corporation, RR-616, 2014. As of July 25, 2018:
https://www.rand.org/pubs/research_reports/RR616.html

Nagel, Joane, and Susan Olzak, "Ethnic Mobilization in New and Old States: An Extension of the Competition Model," *Social Problems*, Vol. 30, No. 2, 1982, pp. 127–143.

Nakash, Yitzhak, *The Shi'is of Iraq*, Princeton, N.J.: Princeton University Press, 1994.

Namaa, Kamal, "Fighting Erupts as Iraq Police Break up Sunni Protest Camp," Reuters, December 30, 2013. As of July 8, 2015:
http://www.reuters.com/article/2013/12/30/
us-iraq-violence-idUSBRE9BT0C620131230

Nasr, S. V. R., "European Colonialism and the Emergence of Modern Muslim States," Oxford Islamic Studies Online, 2016.

Nasr, Vali R., "International Politics, Domestic Imperatives, and Identity Mobilization Sectarianism in Pakistan, 1979–1998," *Comparative Politics*, Vol. 32, No. 2, 2000, pp. 171–190.

———, "When the Shiites Rise," *Foreign Affairs*, Vol. 85, No. 4, 2006, pp. 58–71, 73–74.

———, *The Shi'a Revival*, New York: W. W. Norton and Company, 2007.

Neep, Daniel, *Occupying Syria Under the French Mandate: Insurgency, Space and State Formation*, Cambridge, UK: Cambridge University Press, 2012

Neriah, Jacques, "Egypt's Shiite Minority: Between the Egyptian Hammer and the Iranian Anvil," Jerusalem Center for Public Affairs, September 23, 2012.

Nir, Omri, "The Sunni-Shi'i Balance in Light of the War in Syria and Regional Changes," Rubin Center for Research in International Affairs, April 7, 2014.

Northedge, Alistair, "Al-Iraq al-Arabi: Iraq's Greatest Region in the Pre-Modern Period," in Reidar Visser and Gareth Stansfield, eds., *An Iraq of Its Regions: Cornerstones of a Federal Democracy?* New York: Columbia University Press, 2008, pp. 151–166.

Notzon, Beth, and Gail Nesom, "The Arabic Naming System," *Science Editor*, Vol. 28, No. 1, 2005. As of June 29, 2015:
http://www.councilscienceeditors.org/wp-content/uploads/v28n1p020-021.pdf

Al-Nusra, "The Group of 'Dawlah'—and the Islamic Ruling Regarding it," SITE translation, March 5, 2015a.

Al-Nusra, "Statement No. 24: Statement Clarifying What Came in the Interview of Sheikh Abu Malik al-Shami, May Allah Preserve Him," translated by SITE, March 15, 2015b.

O'Bagy, Elizabeth, "Syria Update: Assad Targets Sunni Along Syria's Coast," Institute for the Study of War, May 10, 2013.

Ostovar, Afshon, "Iran Has a Bigger Problem Than the West: Its Sunni Neighbors," *Lawfare Blog*, June 7, 2015.

Pelham, Nicolas, *A New Muslim Order: The Shia and the Middle East Sectarian Crisis*, London: I. B. Taurius and Co., 2008.

Perthes, Volker, *The Political Economy of Syria Under Assad*, London: I. B. Taurius and Company, 1997.

Pew Research Center, "Mapping the Global Muslim Population, Appendix C: Data Sources by Country," October 7, 2009. As of June 18, 2015:
http://www.pewforum.org/files/2009/10/datasources.pdf

Phillips, Christopher, "Sectarianism and Conflict in Syria," *Third World Quarterly*, Vol. 36, No. 2, March 24, 2015, p. 357

Pursley, Sara, "'Lines Drawn on an Empty Map': Iraq's Borders and the Legend of the Artificial State (Part 1)," *Jadaliyya*, June 2, 2015. As of June 20, 2015:
http://www.jadaliyya.com/pages/index/21759/
lines-drawn-on-an-empty-map_iraq's-borders-and-the

Al-Qarawee, Harith, "The Rise of Sunni Identity in Iraq," *National Interest*, April 5, 2013. As of June 23, 2015:
http://nationalinterest.org/commentary/sunni-identitys-rise-iraq-8314

Rand, Dafna H., and Nicholas A. Heras, "Iraq's Sunni Reawakening: How to Defeat ISIS and Save the Country," *Foreign Affairs*, March 16, 2015. As of July 1, 2015:
https://www.foreignaffairs.com/articles/iraq/2015-03-16/iraqs-sunni-reawakening

al-Rasheed, Madawi, "Middle East Dictators Feed Sectarianism," *Al-Monitor*, December 15, 2014.

Reese, Aaron, "Sectarian and Regional Conflict in the Middle East," Middle East Security Report 13, Institute for the Study of War, July 2013.

Republic of Iraq, "Iraq's Governorates by Area and Their Relative Share of Area and Population: 1997, 2009," spreadsheet, Ministry of Planning Central Statistical Organization, 2010.

Roberts, John Morris, and Odd Arne Westad, *The History of the World*, New York: Oxford University Press, 2013.

Robinson, Francis, *The Cambridge Illustrated History of the Islamic World*, New York: Cambridge University Press, 1996.

Sahgal, Neha, Pew Research Center, "The Escalating Shi'a-Sunni Conflict: Assessing Arab Public Attitudes," conference address, Stimson Center, Washington, D.C., February 18, 2015.

Sakai, Keiko, "Tribalization as a Tool of State Control in Iraq: Observations on the Army, the Cabinets and the National Assembly," in Faleh Abdul-Jabar and Hosham Dawood, *Tribes and Power: Nationalism and Ethnicity in the Middle East*, London: Saqi Books, 2003, pp. 109–135.

Salamandra, Christa, "Sectarianism in Syria: Anthropological Reflections," *Middle East Critique*, Vol. 22, No. 3, 2013, pp. 303–306.

Salamey, Imad, *The Government and Politics of Lebanon*, London: Routledge, 2013.

Salucci, Ilario, *A People's History of Iraq: The Iraqi Communist Party, Workers' Movements, and the Left 1924–2004*, Chicago: Haymarket Books, 2003 (tr. 2005).

"Saudi Arabia Has a Shiite Problem," *Foreign Policy*, December 3, 2014.

"Saudis Reportedly Funding Iraqi Sunni Insurgents," *USAToday*, December 8, 2006. As of August 16, 2015:
http://usatoday30.usatoday.com/news/world/iraq/
2006-12-08-saudis-sunnis_x.htm

Schenker, David, "Qaradawi and the Struggle for Sunni Islam," *PolicyWatch*, No. 2157, Washington Institute, October 16, 2013.

Schofield, Richard, "Borders, Regions and Time: Defining the Iraqi Territorial State," in Reidar Visser and Gareth Stansfield, eds., *An Iraq of Its Regions: Cornerstones of a Federal Democracy?* New York: Columbia University Press, 2008, pp. 167–204.

Sherlock, Ruth, and Magdy Samaan, "Syria: Full Horror of al-Qubeir Massacre Emerges," *Telegraph*, June 7, 2012.

Shuqir, Shafiq, "At-ta'dud al-'araqi wah ad-dini fi bina' 'Iraq al-mustaqbal" [Ethnic and religious diversity in the composition of the future Iraq], *Al Jazeera*, March 10, 2004. As of June 23, 2015:
http://www.aljazeera.net/specialfiles/pages/
b560023c-4cef-438c-94ff-759a2613e2f8

Simon, Reeva Spector, *Iraq Between the Two World Wars*, New York: Columbia University Press, 2000 (2007 edition).

Simon, Reeva Spector, and Eleanor H. Tajirian, eds., *The Creation of Iraq: 1914–1921*, New York: Columbia University Press, 2004, Kindle.

"Smite Their Necks," video, SITE translation, Hama Province Islamic State, March 28, 2015.

Smyth, Philip, *The Shiite Jihad in Syria and its Regional Effects*, Washington Institute for Near East Policy, Policy Focus 138, 2015.

Sowell, Kurt, "Iraq's Second Sunni Insurgency," Hudson Institute, 2014. As of July 8, 2015:
http://www.hudson.org/research/10505-iraq-s-second-sunni-insurgency

Stewart, Dona J., *The Middle East Today: Political, Geographical and Cultural Perspectives*, New York: Routledge, 2013

"Sykes-Picot Agreement," Encyclopaedia Britannica, May 31, 2016.

"Syria: International Religious Freedom Report 2006," Washington, D.C., U.S. Department of State, 2006.

Syrian Arab Tribes Council, Facebook post, June 5, 2012.

"Takfiri Terrorists Commit Massacre Against Syrian Druze in Idleb Countryside," *al-Manar*, June 11, 2015.

Tharoor, Ihsaan, "Syria's Turkmen Rebels, the Group at the Center of the Russia-Turkey Clash," *Washington Post*, November 24, 2015.

"The Abbasid Dynasty: The Golden Age of Islamic Civilization," Saylor Foundation, 2012.

"The Escalating Shia-Sunni Conflict: Assessing the Role of ISIS," Stimson Center Conference, Middle East Program, December 15, 2014.

"The Future of the Global Muslim Population," Pew Research Center, January 27, 2011.

Totten, Michael J., "Assad Shells Alawite Stronghold," *World Affairs Journal*, August 13, 2011.

Tripp, Charles, *A History of Iraq*, 3rd ed., Cambridge, UK: Cambridge University Press, 2007.

Trofimov, Yaroslav, "Sunni-Shiite Conflict Reflects Modern Power Struggle, Not Theological Schism," *Wall Street Journal*, May 14, 2015a.

———, "To U.S. Allies, al-Qaeda Affiliate in Syria Becomes the Lesser Evil," *Wall Street Journal*, June 11, 2015b.

"Turkey Cracks Down on Foreign Fighters Crossing Border to Join ISIS," CBSnews.com, September 29, 2015.

UN—*See* United Nations.

United Nations, *Universal Declaration of Human Rights*, December 10, 1948. As of February 12, 2011:
http://www.un.org/en/universal-declaration-human-rights/index.html

———, *International Covenant on Civil and Political Rights: General Comment Number 27– Freedom of Movement (Article 12)*, November 2, 1999.

———, *The Human Security Framework and National Human Development Reports: A Review of Experiences and Current Debates*, May 2006.

———, *Iraq: Population (Thousands), Medium Variant, 1950–2100*, Department of Economic and Social Affairs, Population Division, Population Estimates and Projections Section, 2015a. As of June 17, 2015:
http://esa.un.org/wpp/unpp/p2k0data.asp

———, *Data Sources for Population Estimates*, Department of Economic and Social Affairs, Population Division, Population Estimates and Projections Section, 2015b.

United Nations News Centre, "News Focus: Syria," undated. As of March 22, 2016:
http://www.un.org/apps/news/infocusRel.asp?infocusID=146

UN News Centre—*See* United Nations News Centre.

U.S. Central Intelligence Agency, "The World Factbook: Iraq," undated. As of June 17, 2015:
https://www.cia.gov/library/publications/the-world-factbook/geos/iz.html

Van Ostaeyan, Pieter, "Al-Jazeera: Interview with Jabhat al-Nusra Amir Abu-Muhammad al-Julani," blog post, translation, May 27, 2015.

Visser, Reidar, "Two Regions of Southern Iraq," in Reidar Visser and Gareth Stansfield, eds., *An Iraq of Its Regions: Cornerstones of a Federal Democracy?* New York: Columbia University Press, 2008a, pp. 27–50.

———, "Historical Myths of a Divided Iraq," *Survival: Global Politics and Strategy*, Vol. 50, No. 2, 2008b, pp. 95–106.

Visser, Reidar, and Gareth Stansfield, eds., *An Iraq of Its Regions: Cornerstones of a Federal Democracy?* New York: Columbia University Press, 2008.

Walker, Martin, "The Making of Modern Iraq," *Wilson Quarterly*, Vol. 27, No. 2, 2003, pp. 29–40.

Wehrey, Frederic, "The Roots and Future of Sectarianism in the Gulf," Project on Middle East Political Science, March 21, 2014.

Weiss, Bernard, "Interpretation in Islamic Law: The Theory of Ijtihād," *American Journal of Comparative Law*, Vol. 22, No. 6, 1978 [*Proceedings of an International Conference on Comparative Law in Salt Lake City Utah*, February 24–25, 1977], pp. 199–212.

Wieland, Carsten, "The Bankruptcy of Humanism? Primordialism Dominates the Agenda of International Politics," *Internationale Politik und Gesellschaft*, 2005, pp. 142–158. As of March 24, 2016:
http://www.fes.de/ipg/IPG4_2005/10_WIELAND.PDF

Wikipedia, "Anglo-Iraqi Treaty of 1930," last updated June 17, 2018. As of August 3, 2018:
https://en.wikipedia.org/wiki/Anglo-Iraqi_Treaty_of_1930#Full_text

Wimmer, Andreas, "Democracy and Ethno-religious Conflict in Iraq," *Survival: Global Politics and Strategy*, Vol. 45, No. 4, 2007, pp. 111–134.

"World Directory of Minorities and Indigenous Peoples—Turkey: Alevis," United Nations High Commissioner for Refugees, 2008.

World Values Survey, "Wave 5 2005–2008: Results, Iraq 2006, Technical Record," World Values Survey Association, 2014. As of June 18, 2015:
http://www.worldvaluessurvey.org/WVSDocumentationWV5.jsp

Wurmser, David, *Tyranny's Ally: America's Failure to Defeat Saddam Hussein*, Washington, D.C.: American Enterprise Institute Press, 1999.

Yaphe, Judith, "Tribalism in Iraq, the Old and the New," *Middle East Policy*, Vol. 7, No. 3, 2000, pp. 51–58.

Yazbek, Samar, *A Woman in the Crossfire: Diaries of the Syrian Revolution*, trans. Max Weiss, London: Haus Publishing, 2012.

Ziada, Faruq, "Is There a Sunni Majority in Iraq?" *counterpunch*, website, December 27, 2006. As of June 19, 2015:
http://www.counterpunch.org/2006/12/27/is-there-a-sunni-majority-in-iraq/

Zubaida, Sami, "The Fragments Imagine the Nation: The Case of Iraq," *International Journal of Middle East Studies*, Vol. 34, 2002, pp. 205–215.